UNTANGLING THE WEB OF PROFESSIONAL LIABILITY

Design Professionals Insurance Company
Publication
Third Edition

Edward B. Howell
Richard P. Howell

ACKNOWLEDGMENTS

This publication evolves from the experience and research of many individuals: Joseph A. McQuillan and Ruth Wilson deserve special mention. The American Consulting Engineers Council has kindly permitted the inclusion, with modification, of portions of The ACEC Professional Liability Loss Prevention Manual published originally in 1969.

TABLE OF CONTENTS

EXHIBITS

FOREWORD

If ever there was a time for prompt and concerted effort to combat a threat to the design profession, that time is now. The menace is professional liability claims and losses. The subject has been discussed and debated within professional societies for many years. Universal agreement exists on the seriousness of the problem, on the damage of adverse publicity resulting from claims and judgments against design professionals, and on the financial difficulties imposed by liability insurance rates. There is common agreement that something should be done, but so far no common agreement has been reached on **what** should be done.

Errors can never be completely eliminated, nor can claims against design professionals for alleged substandard or negligent performance be barred. No loss prevention program can ethically protect against the institution of meritorious suits for damages or injuries. However, the number of claims can be diminished by: 1) avoiding the causes of claims to the best of human ability; 2) educating the public, the legislative bodies, the courts, and the client so that they understand the responsibilities and duties of professionals; and 3) self-policing so that membership in the professions will mean competence, responsibility and integrity.

This manual places heavy emphasis upon short-term solutions and maximum immediate effect. You are urged to study this document carefully. Take seriously the recommendations it contains, for they are based on the experiences of your fellow design professionals and upon careful expert analysis of the factors underlying liability problems. Most important, use it on your day-to-day practice, and make certain that all of your associates do the same.

INTRODUCTION

We are witnessing what some authorities term a litigation explosion. The private practice of a design professional seems particularly vulnerable. For a design professional to be charged with professional negligence is a serious matter. Even if the action proves unsuccessful or without merit and he is vindicated, the damage to his reputation lingers insidiously.

**Sue them,
then ask questions**

Why has this trend in professional liablility claims emerged? What can the design professional do to fend off this burden which threatens his very existence? In the following pages, a partial answer to these questions may be found. Light will be shed on the "why" of professional liability problems and practical remedies proposed. To shed this light, an examination will be conducted not only of the procedural aspects of his practice but of the very nature of the design professional himself. Reasons for this probing stem from study of the many claims made against design professionals. Most claims can be traced in whole or in part to human factors.

**E and O not
the crux**

Most competent design professional firms are painfully aware of any deficiencies in technical competence existing within their firms. Hence, although elements which influence the accumulation of technical competence and valuable experience will be touched upon, this manual deals primarily with the nontechnical aspects of a practice. Therefore, the sequence and brief rationale of our approach will be as follows:

- Discuss professionalism, for unless a professional understands what his duties and responsibilities are by simply being a professional, he is exposed to liability and may do himself and his colleagues great damage.

- Failures in interpersonal relationships, more than any other consideration, seem to be at the root of conflicts. Therefore, this topic deserves considerable mention.

- Procedures followed in business activities can reduce or extend considerably the exposure of the design professional to professional liability claims. Some of the major problem areas must be dealt with in any quest to reduce exposure.

- Some technical aspects of a design professional's practice time and again are the source of professional liability claims. Failure to recognize these exposures and act to reduce them is inviting unnecessary risk.

- Although all of the elements treated above reduce exposure, losses never can be completely eliminated. The last defense, professional liability insurance, provides a final protective measure which, when utilized in conjunction with the above elements, minimizes professional liability exposure.

The measure of success of any advice depends upon its proper implementation. Hopefully, the results of your efforts will show not only a reduction in damaging claims, but will result in beneficial side effects of smoother business operations as well.

Not so much publicized, but potentially a great source of damage to the quality of design professional work, are state and federal government successes in establishing procurement regulations emphasizing fee structures rather than quality. Of course, any design professional can lower his fee and therefore produce something of poorer quality, but in so doing may serve only a procedural requirement at a long range cost to the public and to professionalism.

Cost benefits seldom accrue from low-bid design work

That design professionals should be singled out for this federal and state onslaught aimed at pitting one design professional against another through competitive bidding might have been predicted since recognition of engineers and architects as professionals has been slow in coming. Moreover, the public is confused by the word "engineer" that is appended euphemistically as a status elevator by misguided industrial relations practitioners to garbage men, janitors, maintenance men, and others pursuing occupations that meet few, if any, of the criteria of professionalism. Because of such confusion, the public will not be prone, as they may be for medical doctors, to rise to the defense of the design professional. Rather, they may overlook his great design achievements and select him as the scapegoat for environmental problems. The existing and pending legislation that may handcuff the design professional has been triggered by a handful of alleged bribers who, like Judas goats, have brought the legislative wrath down on the design profession.

Rat killer — an extermination engineer

Mr. Morris Llewellyn Cooke was most prophetic when in 1918 he declared:

> *Until we engineers can place the service of humanity as the significant and dominant plank in our platform, the profession will continue to have the status of the hired servant, and veer here and there as the winds of business and other special interests may dictate.*

[1] *The Consulting Engineer*, February 1975, p. 8.

It is clear that the very concept of professionalism is under challenge. The symptoms are escalating lawsuits and increasing infringement by government either through statutes or through regulating agencies. This challenge must be met. But to meet it, it is of paramount importance that the professional:

- clearly understands who he is;

- knows how his status evolved; and

- comprehends what, as a professional, his duties and responsibilities are.

Responsibility and authority

B. A Professional — Who Is He?

In defining the terms profession and professionalism, the main dilemma is the overlap in their meaning with craft, trade, occupation, vocation, calling, or employment. For example, Penn Kimball states, "Among those who gather, write and edit the news for a living, the highest compliment is to be called a 'pro.' It is the mark of a respected journeyman in a demanding craft."[2] In making this statement, Kimball equates the meaning of pro, i.e., professional, with journeyman, and, indirectly, craft.

Professional connotations

Falling back to the most authoritative sources of the English language, Webster for the American English and the British Oxford, definitions of profession and professionalism remain unclear.

In Webster, the definition of profession nearest to our understanding is: "A calling requiring specialized knowledge and often long and intensive academic preparation." But it is also, "A principal calling, vocation, or employment," and ". . . a whole body of persons engaged in a calling." With Oxford, the definition is even broader: ". . . vocation, calling, esp. one that involves some branch of learning or science, as the learned professions (divinity, law, medicine)." However, it can also be, ". . . the military profession," or ". . . a carpenter by profession."

[2]Kenneth S. Lynn, Ed., and the Editors of *Daedalus*, "Journalism — Art, Craft or Profession" (Boston: Houghton Mifflin Company, 1965), p. 242.

Morris L. Cogan defines a profession as follows:

A profession is a vocation whose practice is founded upon an understanding of the theoretical structure of some department of learning or science, and upon the abilities accompanying such understanding. This understanding and these abilities are applied to the vital practical affairs of man. The practices of the profession are modified by knowledge of a generalized nature and by the accumulated wisdom and experience of mankind, which serve to correct the errors of specialism. The profession, serving the vital needs of man, considers its first ethical imperative to be altruistic service to the client.[3]

Many who call themselves design professionals may take exception to the altruistic service part of this definition if they, in their own minds, equate altruism with philanthropy. However, when altruism is considered in the sense of definition by Webster "... regard for, or devotion to, the interests of others," few, if any, professionals would quibble.

Clearly, ten philologists, or laymen for that matter, in defining what might constitute professionalism would derive ten different definitions. Popular etymology is at work — the changing of meaning by degrees based on the use by the populus. As a result, in descending order of status, we find such new expressions emerging as: true professional, paraprofessional, subprofessional, quasiprofessional, nonprofessional, and pseudoprofessional — the last two having derogatory connotations.

C. The Evolution of Professionalism

Professionals may have always existed but have been recognized as "professionals" for only a few centuries at most. According to the Oxford Shorter Dictionary, the earliest connotation of the adjective "professed" was: "That has taken the vows of a

[3]Wagner, H.A., "Principles of Professional Conduct in Engineering," *The Annals of the American Academy of Political and Social Sciences*, 197 (January 1955), pp. 46-52.

religious order." By 1675, the meaning was secularized, "That professes to be duly qualified; professional."

A. M. Carr-Sanders, probably the first English professor to analyze systematically the transition of occupations to professions, gave perspective to "The Professions" in a 1928 Herbert Spencer lecture delivered at Oxford.

It is of some of the problems connected with the evolution of new professions and with the changes that have come over the older professions that I wish to speak today. To bring these problems more clearly into light it may be well very briefly to review the course of events during the last two centuries. In 1711, Addison referred to the three great professions of divinity, law, and physic.

*Even at that time the profession of physic was in process of evolution. The apothecaries were assuming some of the functions of the physicians, and persons who, towards the end of the century came to be known as chemists and druggists, were encroaching upon the field of the apothecaries. New professions were arising. In 1665 Pepys recorded of his wife: 'she had a fore tooth drawn out to-day which do trouble me.' The operator was a barber surgeon and master of his Company. In the following century Beardmore seems to have been what we now call a dentist and to have acted as dentist-in-ordinary to George III. But change was not yet swift. As late as 1838 a writer in **Tait's Magazine** says that 'dentistry, as we find it called is growing into a profession.' It was not until the nineteenth century was some way advanced that new professions began to achieve recognition in rapid succession. The first half of the century saw the rise of the dentists, veterinary surgeons, engineers, and architects. The Royal College of Veterinary Surgeons obtained a charter in 1844 while the Royal Institute of British Architects dates from 1834. The civil engineers, so calling themselves in distinction to military engineers, began to be* heard of towards the end of the eighteenth century. The Institution of Civil Engineers was founded in 1818, Thomas Telford being the first president. The Institution of Mechanical Engineers, of which George Stephenson was the first president, dates from 1847. Meanwhile the evolution of the medical profession continued. The Apothecaries' Act was passed in 1815 and John Keats was one of the first persons licensed under that Act. The Apothecaries ultimately became the general practitioners, and the unity of the medical profession was achieved by the Medical Act of 1858.

Theodore Caplow identifies five steps involved in the evolution of a profession.

The first step is the establishment of a professional association, with definite membership criteria designed to keep out the unqualified.

Professional progression

The second step is the change of name, which serves the multiple function of reducing identification with the previous occupational status, asserting a technological monopoly, and providing a title which can be monopolized, the former one being usually in the public domain.

The third step is the development and promulgation of a code of ethics which asserts the social utility of the occupation, sets up public welfare rationale, and develops rules which serve as further criteria to eliminate the unqualified and unscrupulous. The adoption of a code of ethics, despite certain hypocrisies, imposes a real and permanent limitation on internal competition.

The fourth step is a prolonged political agitation, whose object it is to obtain the support of the public power for the maintenance of the new occupational barriers. In practice this usually proceeds by stages from the limitation of a specialized title to those who have passed an examination (registered engineer, certified public accountant) to the final stage at which mere doing of the acts reserved to the profession is a crime.

Concurrent with this activity, which may extend over a very long period of time, goes the development of training facilities directly or indirectly controlled by the professional society, particularly with respect to admission and to final qualification; the establishment through legal action of certain privileges of confidence and inviolability, the elaboration of the rules of decorum found in the code, and the establishment — after conflict — of working relations with related professional groups.[4]

D. Duties and Responsibilities

Protect your own?

Once a profession is established, the tendency is for the members of the profession to rest on their laurels. For example, in one recent year, only about one medical doctor in 10,000 had his license to practice revoked or was forced out of the medical society. Such failure to police one's ranks not only results in lowering standards of performance but it also provides the plaintiff's bar with a valid argument for the contingency fee practice. Although acknowledging that lawyers may end up with over 50% of the professional liability money awarded, the plaintiff's attorneys point out that they alone are doing an effective job of weeding out the professional misfit. Therefore, design professionals have the duty and responsibility to their profession and to society to maintain technical and ethical standards among their members through adequate enforcement measures.

E. Formation of Attitudes in Others

Is there any correlation between the number of claims brought against a design professional and the amount of time he spends creating a professional image in the eyes of others? Yes, there is. With a little reflection you can think of the name of a colleague who invariably seems to gather the respect of all of those who come in contact with him. He seems to engender a feeling of confidence in his clients and generally has a reputation for producing

[4]*Harvard Educational Review,* Winter 1955.

consistently complete and high quality design services. You have heard others say of him, "He is what I consider to be a true professional."

Since the creation of a professional image leads to a reduction in claims, let us examine how this image is acquired. As mentioned previously, traditionally a man who was considered to be a member of a profession was either a lawyer, a physician, or a clergyman. Then, as now, great emphasis was placed upon a high sense of duty, public service, ethics, and civic responsibility. Later, other disciplines outside of medicine, religion, or law joined the ranks of the professionals by way of legal statutes establishing minimum standards and by hard-won public acceptance over a period of years. The design professionals are included in this latter group. One big difference remains. The average individual rarely has a requirement for the design professional's services comparable to the services required of a doctor, lawyer, or clergyman. Because of your remoteness in the eyes of the average citizen, you must devote extra effort to create and maintain the image of a professional. This includes emphasizing your sense of duty, public service, ethics, and civic responsibility in all that you do.

Perhaps you have noticed that the same man who is highly respected is also rarely involved in litigation and has far fewer claims brought against him than others. In comparing yourself with him you may be puzzled to note that, in your opinion, you have equal if not greater technical competence than he. What attribute about him makes it unthinkable for his client to question any aspect of the work he has performed? The answer in part is his professional image. If you can cultivate and maintain in your client and the contractor their admiration and respect for you and their belief that you are above all else a professional, the result will be fewer claims brought against you.

Consider a project you are currently working on. If a serious problem should arise at the job site, or if something should go wrong and the contractor points the finger at you, how will the client react? Whose

Out of sight, out of mind

11

side of the argument will the client favor? If the client is faced with added expense, will he be more apt to listen with sympathy to your story or will you find yourself confronted with a lawsuit? The attitude your client has toward you and his appreciation of your efforts in his behalf relate closely to his general attitude toward you and thus the likelihood of a claim against you.

The formation of the attitude that you are, above all, a professional leads to great benefits in dealing with a contractor. In addition, your personnel should also convey this idea. Are your employees, who come in contact with contractors, aware that their personal conduct has a tremendous influence on the frequency and type of claims arising out of construction review? It would be well to remember that contractors should always think of you as a gentleman (even if a "tough" gentleman).

Thus the formation of attitudes in others of what a professional is — and more important **that you are a professional** — relies on what you have done to foster that idea. The result of "nurturing a good attitude" is a healthy, growing fence between you and professional liability claims.

F. Summary

Professionals are an endangered species. Although to achieve their elevated status they labored literally for centuries, today we endure an era in which forces are at work that are bent on defaming the stature and eliminating the special privileges of the professional. The success of these forces stems from abject failure by professionals to comprehend their stakehold — their role and heritage — and to convey this to clients and others. To be credible, such communication must be accompanied by an unmasking of charlatans — purging a few rotten apples in the barrel — in order to not only annul the demise of professionalism but also to avoid unnecessary exposure to professional liability claims. Guilt by association is a persuasive influence. The time is ripe, if not overdue, to deliberately adopt a defensive stance, to make plain to the public what they too have at stake in professionalism and to move forward once again in professionally serving mankind with quality designs.

II
interpersonal relationships

If you expect to find a single volume, be prepared for a shock. The dictionary covers several shelves. In fact, there are 47 volumes of about 700 pages each — over 30,000 pages of court-determined definitions.

An analysis of this dictionary reveals that some words are often the crux of lawsuits and other words seldom are involved. Take, for example, the word "final." Interpretations of this word require about 50 pages. Clearly, it is a word to be avoided in your communications. If we seek to categorize words that often end up in this dictionary, we find they fall into a pattern:

- Extreme words, such as "final"
- Words of multiple meaning
- Words of promise

a. Our Black or White World

This pattern evidently describes something about human behavior. It seems ingrained that we all tend to use extreme words. In the process, we demonstrate a general laxity in communication. For example, we can speak of a person as moral or immoral when, in reality, he is neither. We can agree to maximize, minimize, or optimize without blinking an eyelid. We accept words like any, all, none, full, equal, and various forms of the verb "to be" in our brochures, contracts, or proposals, without qualification. It is the way we are.

Have you been asked to sign an agreement with clauses such as the following?

The Design Professional shall assist the Owner in applying for and obtaining, from **all** applicable public agencies, **all** permits, approvals, or waivers required by law.

The Design Professional shall prepare at the conclusion of **each** phase of the work a **complete** estimate of the project costs.

The Design Professional agrees to defend, indemnify, and save harmless the Owner, its officers, agents, and employees, from and against **any** and **all** claims arising out of the acts, errors, or omissions of the Design Professional or the Owner.

If so, your first clue to trouble would be recognizing the unwarranted use of extreme words. Often, the owner did not intend to impose the impossible conditions on you that such words imply. He would not object to your modifying the clauses. Take the first clause above. You might modify it as follows:

The Design Professional shall assist the Owner in applying for and obtaining permits and approvals normally required by law. This assistance shall not extend to the preparation of environmental impact reports, research studies, special documentation, or special tests. Such services, if required, shall be compensated for as Additional Services.

The problems inherent to the next two clauses, above, will be discussed in subsequent chapters.

b. The Mush of Meaning

The multiple meaning of words is a fact we cannot escape. Simple little words sometimes have dozens of meanings. Look up the word "tap." Another little one that befuddles foreigners who are intent on learning our language is "get." Having looked up these two three-letter words may make it easier for you to believe the fact that our 500 most commonly used words have 14,000 meanings!

Small wonder that the courts are often called upon to determine what words mean. Two words that have a different connotation for design professionals than for others and that have often been defined by courts are "inspect" and "supervise." They appear so often in the *Dictionary of Words and Phrases* that they should be viewed defensively by design professionals. Watch how the court's definitions of these words can entangle you in a word-web:

> There is no substantial difference between services of "superintendence" and of "inspection."

> The words "supervise," "superintend," and "oversee" in ordinary use and common acceptance have substantially the same meaning.

Etymological entrapment

> "Control" is the power or authority to manage, direct, superintend, restrict, regulate, govern, administer, or oversee.

> The terms "direct" and "administer" are synonymous. Both mean to manage, control, and conduct affairs of business.

Clearly, the entanglement grows as the courts decide that "inspect" and "supervise" mean:

Superintend	Restrict
Oversee	Regulate
Control	Govern
Manage	Administer
Direct	Conduct

Are these what you mean when you agree to inspect or supervise construction? If not, beware!

c. Can Do

Man is optimistic. This characteristic seems innate. In the harsh world of our distant ancestors, perhaps optimism was essential in order to face the dangers that abounded.

Optimism is reflected in the things we say and do. For example, the *Lorge* magazine count of the frequency of words used (4.5 million words) found that optimistic words (e.g., better compared with worse, or advance rather than retreat) were employed about four times as frequently as their antonyms.

Do you fail to fasten your seatbelt? Most people do, despite the overwhelming evidence of its value.

Technical professionals probably are more optimistic than others. Placing a man on the surface of the moon was not achieved by nay sayers, but by can doers.

But beware! The man who was placed on the moon arrived years after the original, planned date. A study of major systems conducted by Stanford Research Institute (now SRI International) found a two-thirds year slippage for each year scheduled. In other words, an average schedule would be more accurate if multiplied by 1.66.

Techniques to avoid being entrapped in this web of optimism are covered in the next chapter (Estimating Costs and Schedules), but there are also words that should be red flagged to avoid optimistic pitfalls. Some are optimistic words of promise like guarantee, warrant, certify, ensure, insure, etc. Avoid these. Usually someone is asking you to assume the role of risk-taker. That is not your role. Be pragmatic.

The most common words that bind you — often into optimistic promises — are the words "will" and "shall." A caution light should flash each time you encounter these words. Often, they may be softened by changing from the imperative to the permissive (e.g., "shall" to "may").

d. Some Communication Facilitators

Three techniques may help avoid becoming entangled in lawsuits over word meanings:

- Finding more exact words
- Paraphrase and disavow
- Seek feedback

There are about 600,000 English words. You, as an average design professional, employ only about 2,000 in your day-to-day conversation. Substitute more exact· words. Make an ally of Webster.

An example of the paraphrase and disavowal technique follows:

Inspection, when used by the design professional, *means* visual observation of materials, equipment, or construction work, on an intermittent basis, to determine that the work is in substantial conformance with the contract documents and the design intent.

Such inspection *does not* constitute acceptance of the work, *nor* shall it be construed to relieve the contractor in any way from his responsibility for the means and methods of construction or for safety on the construction site.

Since most English words have varying connotations, a good method for testing oral communication is to have your listener feedback the communication to you in his own words. The engineers, architects, and contractors, as members of a team effort must seek to think and act as a unit. Any ambiguities or misunderstandings which exist within this team can easily lead to errors, delays, and, sometimes, litigation. The following case illustrates the type of claim which results from poor communication.

A very conscientious Midwestern design professional visited a construction site to observe the progress on an underground sewer system being installed to serve the project under construction. The scheduling of this portion of the work was particularly critical. His design called for connection of the new service to an existing sewer main. Interruption in service to other buildings nearby had to be minimized. The design professional carefully reviewed the contractor's work. To his dismay he discovered the type of joints being used between sections of piping were not the kind specified, nor were they, in his opinion, suitable for the application. Realizing prompt action might prevent delay and further wasted effort by the contractor, he rushed to the general contractor's shack at the site. In a loud, urgent manner the design professional instructed the superintendent to "Stop the work immediately and wait for further instructions!" With no further explanation the design professional left the site. His excited state and tone of voice communicated much more to the contractor's superintendent than his actual words. The superintendent knew that on this particular project the design professional had been granted authority by the owner to give "stop work" instructions affecting the *entire* project in addition to those areas relating to the design professional's design. Naturally confused, the superintendent believed the design professional wished to cease work on the entire project and he took immediate steps to do so. Of course, the intent of the design professional was to stop work on the

It is not what you do, but how you do it that counts

new sewer *only*. The resulting delay cost the owner considerable waste of time and money.

The design professional firmly believed his instructions were sufficiently clear, and that the superintendent, for some reason, deliberately chose to misinterpret his intent. The real problem was a breakdown in understanding stemming from incomplete and unclear transmission of information. The resulting claim against this design professional was self-induced, that is, brought about by his own actions. His motives were the best, but his communication was poor.

This simple example illustrates how difficult it is to know exactly what we are communicating to others. Had the design professional asked the superintendent to repeat his instructions, they might have discovered the misunderstanding and avoided a costly delay.

3. And Now, The Written Word

In addition to the general oral communication rules already suggested, there are other, more specific remedies which you can implement in your office to improve effective written communication and thus help to prevent claims.

First, all correspondence leaving the office which concerns projects or plans should be reviewed by designated principals. It takes experience to learn how to be careful about the written word. In general, principals have developed this skill. Their review of correspondence usually will result in corrections, clarifications, and improvements. It provides a cross-check system for discovering misstatements and misunderstandings. Such review will produce:

Review

a) Correspondence of a higher quality. If an employee is aware that his letters will be reviewed, he naturally takes more care in his writing.

b) Elimination of ambiguities.

c) Elimination of errors, including grammatical. This also will generally improve the design professional's image.

d) Reduction in the risk of defamation suits involving libel or slander.

The firm's principals can also review each other's correspondence.

4. How About Specifications?

Defining your engineering jargon

Do contractors routinely seek clarification and direction after reading one of your specifications? If so, this may indicate that your specifications contain ambiguous or obscure provisions. An excellent remedy is to include a glossary or definition section. Dozens of words are repeatedly used in specifications which should either be defined or replaced with words of a more precise meaning. For example, how often do you use the three words "furnish," "install," and "provide" interchangeably, intending that they all mean the same? Check their meaning and you will discover considerable differences. In Webster's Dictionary you will find that "install" means to place, establish, settle or fix in a position; "furnish" means to supply, provide or give; and "provide" means to supply, furnish, or make available. As one can see, "install" does not convey the meaning that the item to be installed is to be supplied by the same party installing it. Nor do the words "furnish" and "provide" connote that after an item is supplied, it will also be fixed in place.

It is amazing the number of words used by design professionals which have very special and limited meanings. The average layman finds it virtually impossible to understand the subtle distinctions between these special words. For many of these words there is no one standard definition. A comprehensive knowledge of the scope and boundaries encompassed by such words is learned through long experience. To complicate matters, even the same disciplines located in different geographical areas assign different meanings to the same words. Little wonder a lay member of a jury has difficulty grasping the intent of one who specifies, for example, that a particular fume hood shall have "all standard options as required for satisfactory performance."

Some words are so susceptible to misinterpretation and so difficult to explain to a jury that it is wiser to substitute another word or phrase to describe a particular activity. Consider the following examples:

Engineering Jargon	Preferable Word (or Words)	Risky words
Approve	Review (See also recommended wording used on Shop Drawing Stamp Examples)	
Inspection	Construction Review	
Supervision	Construction Observation	
Or Equal	Or Equivalent	
Satisfactory Operation	Operation as specified	

HOW WORD MEANINGS VARY

Approve

a. Special Meaning Intended — To give limited, or conditional, or qualified permission to use material, equipment, or methods; the conditions being strict compliance with contract document requirements.

b. Dictionary Definition — 1. To sanction, consent to, *confirm*, ratify. 2. To be favorable toward, think or declare to be good.

c. Laymen's Meaning — Unqualified acceptance.

d. Professional Liability Implications — Judge and jury have a tendency to view limited approval with suspicion and have on occasion considered it a waiver of the original requirements, and tend to disregard any limitations.

Or Equal

a. Special Meaning Intended — To possess the same performance qualities and characteristics and fulfill the utilitarian function without any decrease in quality, durability, or longevity. *No* inference that items must be identical in *all* respects if above conditions are satisfied.

b. Dictionary Definition — Of the same quantity, size, number, value, degree, intensity.

c. Laymen's Meaning — The items are identical in all respects without any difference.

d. Professional Liability Implications — Judge and jury sometimes tend to view the design professional's acquiescence in use of an item which is not identical to that specified as a waiver of original requirements.

Ambiguity and the contractor's responsibility

Instruct your specifications proofreaders to maintain a continual search for words that have more than one meaning. Most words do — in fact some have dozens of meanings and an almost equal number of connotations. Therefore, if there is any doubt about the meaning, choose a different word or define the word in a glossary or specification definition section. Be especially cautious with words you use to outline the scope of a contractor's responsibility. Remember, contractors who understand your specifications have the tendency to remove any fat from their bid figure. On the other hand, contractors who must guess what your intent is may feel compelled to assign a higher cost to the project than might otherwise be the case.

Finally, review the specification yourself before it is issued, bearing in mind the maxim that **any portion of a specification which can possibly be subject to more than one interpretation is incorrectly written.**

5. Drawing Symbol Lists, Legends, and Notes

Drawings which are complete and easy to follow are essential. Why? Because in most cases, the workman at the job site is provided with a set of drawings but rarely sees the specifications. This preference by workmen for the visual plan of work — the drawing — must be considered in determining the contents of a drawing. In short, drawings must be accurate and comprehensive.

Most of us would agree that an understanding of abbreviations is a key to reading every set of drawings. Yet, many drawings without symbol lists or legends reach the field, presenting an unwelcome problem to the workmen. Legends are rarely omitted by those design professional firms who fully recognize their value in reducing claims.

A good practice to establish in your office is that no dimensions, quantities, or capacities are shown on the drawings in more than one place. Then any subsequent changes must be made only once and the likelihood of conflicting information is eliminated.

Civil engineers and land surveyors expose themselves to claims when underground utilities are shown on survey maps. Almost without exception, the intent is for the contractor to verify the exact location of all underground utilities at a site before commencing work. Often such underground utilities are merely transcribed onto drawings from public records. To prevent an unfair burden on the contractor, many firms include a note of explanation prominently located on the drawing. One in common use states:

The locations of existing underground utilities are shown in an approximate way only. The contractor shall determine the exact location of all existing utilities before commencing work. He agrees to be fully responsible for any and all damages which might be occasioned by his failure to exactly locate and preserve any and all underground utilities.

This warning permits the contractor to include in his bid a sufficient allowance to cover the cost of any exploratory excavations needed to verify utility locations.

The drawings and specifications you present to the contractor or workmen are the reflection of your image

Keep in mind that the image you project to the contractor or the workmen results from your drawings and specifications. If the documents are difficult to comprehend, those trying to understand will have a low evaluation of you. But if you smooth their jobs, they will respond in kind should a tight situation develop. Frequently it is the little things in construction that give rise to the big claims. Make certain that your symbols, legends, and notes are not the little things that cause trouble.

6. Contacts, Discussions, Conferences

Have you ever wondered why you lost a valued client? Or why some contractors seem particularly hostile? Or why one of your most competent professionals became dissatisfied and moved to another firm? What went wrong? Perhaps, without realizing it, you have given them the impression "I cannot be bothered running around, holding the contractor's hand, giving the client a short course in construction, or conducting a perpetual training program for employees who ought to know what they are doing. I have enough trouble meeting my deadlines." You communicate with others not only verbally, but also by your actions. Your conduct, therefore, may give a completely erroneous impression of your attitude toward others. Most design professionals are quite willing to answer any reasonably direct question the contractor may have. It would be rare to find a design professional who would not welcome the opportunity to discuss with a client the relative merits of one type of system as compared with another. But how often do you *seek* the opportunity on your own initiative to communicate with these individuals?

To fill such communications gaps, plan regularly scheduled meetings with your employees, clients, and contractors. On large projects, some joint informal meetings are scheduled on a weekly basis between representatives of the contractor, the client, and the design professional.

These sessions can often pinpoint construction problems before they occur, permitting solutions satisfactory to all without the crisis atmosphere.

At the opposite end of the communications spectrum are the design professionals who, although willing to give information to the contractor, do so at the wrong times. One repeated source of claims stems from telephone information given to contractors during bidding. Instruct your personnel, therefore, to refrain from giving oral interpretations of drawings or specifications even if the contractor points out an obvious error. Rather, send written addenda to *all* contractors bidding. Should it be too late to issue an addendum before bid time, it is better to tell the contractor to make his own interpretation without your assistance. Spell out methods in the bid documents by which the contractor may qualify his bid if clarifications by addenda are unavailable. Then, when questions do arise, you can refer the contractor to the bid documents for the proper procedures to use.

For interoffice communications, require all office discussions involving design to be documented by a brief memorandum (see Exhibit 1), a copy to be filed in an appropriate place. Plan weekly progress review conferences on a formal or informal basis for each project. Make it mandatory that project professionals recount their progress over the past week, list problems yet to be

You communicate with others not only by what you say, but also by what you do

Bid pressure and communications

solved, and make requests for whatever information is necessary but has not been received. Periodic reports of this type serve also as a diary of project progress. (See Exhibit 2.)

Written progress reports to a client are immensely valuable. When accompanied by a personal visit, they can be a bond that will keep the client and the professional working together when adversity strikes. Nothing demonstrates a professional approach as effectively as the well-planned, timely transmission of information in an understandable fashion.

EXHIBIT 1

CONFERENCE MEMORANDUM
P. D. & Q., Inc.

Project: VERY TALL OFF. BLDG.   Conference Location: P.D.&Q. OFFICES

Location: ILLINOIS CITY   Parties Present: JOHN DOE

Client: JOHN DOE, ARCHITECT   JAMES OWNER

Date: 5/10/79   RICHARD ROE

Copy to Each Party Present: (Yes)   No

Item:

1. Discussed problem on 17th floor mezz. The present floor-to-floor dimension does not permit the installation of the mezz. due to restricted height. Because the 17th floor will also contain an auditorium. Mr. Doe proposed to make an exception and double the floor-to-floor dimensions on this level. This proposal was accepted by Mr. Owner, subject to review of schematic drawings of the proposed revision.

EXHIBIT 2

PERIODIC PROGRESS REPORT
P. D. & Q., Inc.

Project: Very Tall Office Bldg.   Copies To: _____

Location: Illinois City   Mr. John Doe, Architect

Client: John Doe   Mr. James Owner

Date: 5/12/79

1. We received the approved Schematic Design phase drawings 5/11/79 and are proceeding immediately on the Design Development phase as requested by the architect, John Doe.

2. The problem of the floor space assigned for the mezzanine level, 17th floor, was resolved on 5/10/76 and prints of the final arrangement XA-12 through XA-17 will be marked with our comments and sent back to the architect before 5/15/79.

C. Contacts with Others

As indicated in Chapter I, the contacts that you, the design professional, have with others greatly affect how your claims record reads.

1. Public

The lack of knowledge concerning your duties and responsibilities may result in strange, costly, and tragic occurrences. For example, defending a lawsuit which really has no basis is not only strange, it can be very costly in both time and money and be tragic in its loss of reputation based on the old adage "Where there is smoke, there is fire."

Failure to make other people understand what you do as design professionals results in a staggering number of claims. Consider the following example and you will see why. If an owner must pay extra for an item you left off drawings or out of the specifications, he may sue you to recoup his losses. Often it may be that it was your considered judgment that the item, after some deliberation, be omitted. Yet later, as construction develops, the circumstances may have changed. It may now seem more reasonable, in your judgment, to add the item to the project as extra work. When you made your original decision you may have satisfied the legal standard of care. The owner, with his increased cost, then proceeds to misunderstand your duties. One basis of his complaint is likely to be that you were negligent in originally omitting the item. Another allegation may be that you implied a warranty that the drawings would be complete and, without exception, fit and sufficient for the purpose intended. Neither of these allegations may be true. Yet, because your professional role was misunderstood, you must undergo lengthy litigation.

How much value do you assign to telephone courtesy? Do your personnel who regularly answer the telephone present a cheerful yet businesslike image to the caller? Do you place calls yourself, or do you have your secretary contact the other party before you get on the line? Do your telephone answering personnel refuse to tell the caller whether or not you are in and then insist that the caller give his name before they will pass the call to you? These seemingly inconsequential modes of telephone conduct can have a serious effect on your firm's relationships with the public and with your clients.

It takes relatively little time to review the telephone techniques employed by all of your personnel who are authorized to make and to take calls on behalf of the firm. The involuntary antagonism produced by a lack of courtesy on the telephone can lead to the loss of a client, or sow the seed of a controversy leading to a charge of professional incompetence. Some firms, conscious of the public relations and client relations value of telephone courtesy, establish written guidelines for telephone answering personnel, supplemented by periodic emphasis to impress upon them the high regard the firm holds for this attribute.

A rash of suits has recently been experienced arising out of persons injured at the construction site. Again, why? Because people really do not understand your role as a design professional. They honestly believe you have an active part in determining the contractor's safety precautions.

This brief review of how suits originate against you should help to bring home the point that unfortunate things can happen when people do not understand what you are and what you do. Others, even other design professionals, are not going to explain to the public what your function is. It is up to you to do this.

What can be done? Must you become a public speaker? A teacher? A writer? Is it not more important to pay attention to your work, the principal source of your income? Certainly you cannot entirely give up your profession to become a public educator, but one thing is certain; there is a pressing need for improvement in that area described by that well-worn term *public relations*, of which education is a major part.

Are you a member of any organizations *outside* your profession? Have you ever given a talk before an organization, school class, or a civic group and attempted to explain what your work is? Do you look for ways to tell people what your contribution is to the construction industry? Before you blame others for your professional liability problems, make sure you are doing everything within your power to prevent them.

One claims-free design professional who actively participates in several nonengineering organizations accounts for his involvement by this explanation: "If you want to be a professional, act like one."

Furthermore, do not forget that the "public" may not only become your client, they may also become the jury in a lawsuit against you. The better they understand you, the greater the possiblity of a reasonable verdict.

2. Client

The same methods of approach used in your contacts with the public apply to those with the client. In addition, there are others.

Each time you make a cost estimate for a client, you run the risk of a lawsuit. Why? Because the purpose for which you made it is misunderstood. The client may mistakenly believe that your estimate is a guaranteed maximum figure and budget accordingly. If the final cost exceeds your estimate, he may then allege that you were negligent or that you implicitly warranted its accuracy.

In your relations with a client, never make the mistake of overestimating his knowledge of your duties and procedures. It may seem inconceivable to you that a client may labor under the impression that you control the manufacture of every item you specify. Yet time after time claims are made against design professionals arising out of equipment failure, usually after the standard guarantee periods given by the construction contractor and equipment manufacturer have expired. The uninformed client presented with a financial crisis can well be expected to turn to the designer to recover his losses. Because he does not understand what you were retained to do, he may allege that you were negligent in your equipment selection or that you should have tested it before you specified it.

3. Contractor

A manual may help indoctrinate new personnel

Your contacts, and those of your employees, with the contractors are of utmost importance. Whether you use specially qualified employees to handle all outside construction review problems or you require each of your project managers to conduct the construction review on his own project, more satisfactory results can be obtained by requiring field personnel to follow recommended procedures for the various situations which commonly arise during construction review. One method of achieving acceptable behavior by your personnel is through the use of an indoctrination manual. The manual, drawn up along lines similar to the formal office policy statements used by some firms, contains precautionary directions that reduce the risk of legal entanglements. Such a manual, when written by personnel with long experience in the field who have successfully dealt with job problems and contractor's personnel, can reduce your exposure to claims significantly.

At least three problem areas might be included in the manual:

Important problem areas

a. **Arguing.** Statements made in the heat of anger may lead to defamation suits. Moreover,

40

they inevitably increase hostility and reduce cooperation levels between the parties involved.

b. **Trading.**   Never induce a contractor to perform extra work — made necessary by an omission or error in the drawings and specifications — by allowing him, in return, to omit another specified requirement. Experience indicates that the owner suffers a disservice by such bargaining. Often the cost of the extra work is far less than the value of the work omitted.

c. **The gratuitous undertaking.**   Be wary of your field personnel giving the contractor more information than is required of them. This volunteered sharing of the contractor's work may lead to a sharing of liability for the contractor's performance. The normal function of your personnel does not include directing the activities of the contractor or his workmen. Although a cooperative relationship between the contractor and your employees is always desirable, the present legal climate precludes the "good samaritan" policy by your personnel from having a place on a construction site.

One firm has devised procedures which eliminate some of the problems mentioned above. The firm grants its construction review personnel *no* authority to make any changes to the contract documents. All changes, without exception, must be channeled through the client. At the beginning of the construction phase of each project, a meeting is held with the client or his representative, the general contractor and his superintendent, and the design professional and his field representative. At the conclusion of this meeting, the general contractor is required to sign several copies of a letter which states that he understands that the design professional's field representative has no power to authorize changes. A copy of the signed letter is sent to the client, and a copy is retained by the design professional. This firm is convinced that "the procedure has saved us thousands of dollars by avoiding misunderstandings."

You can see that the maintenance of harmonious relations with the public, your clients, the contractors and the projection of a friendly image in your daily contacts with others can help you turn a potential claimant into an ally.

D. Behavior Under Stress

1. A Gathering Storm

It was not going to be a routine on-site inspection this time. Word had just reached the design professional that the contractor had deviated widely from the requirements on the drawings and specifications. "Why today?" he muttered. "I've had just about all I can take with this job. Yesterday it was the owner — as though **I** could have kept the truckers from striking — and now **this**. That guy is the best contractor in town. What happened to him? This bit is going to cost me my hide."

Human beings under conditions of stress do not act or react rationally

At the site, the contractor was in no better mood. Nervously pacing back and forth, not wearing his hard hat, he was obviously a man under great pressure. He was vaguely aware that his instructions to his crew had not been particularly clear and that he was preoccupied and physically careless to the point of inviting an accident.

Then he saw the design professional's car screech to a halt. Just from the way he got out of the car and slammed the door, the contractor knew there was trouble, and he got ready for the onslaught. This had been a tricky job with a lot of unforeseeable snags — only that morning he had been notified that the delivery of urgently needed parts would be delayed. And then there was the problem at home . . . the sudden appearance of old symptoms, visits to specialists, agonizing uncertainty. He had enough on his mind without hassling with a temperamental design professional.

So they will face each other — the design professional and the contractor. Inevitably, the problems burdening each of them — which may or may not be recognized — will direct the tone, and perhaps even the content, of their encounter. Is either one of these emotionally charged men capable of dealing with the mutual problem that confronts them?

2. Statement of the Problem

Professionals in the construction industry, faced with the growing threat of professional liability claims, can no longer disregard the interdisciplinary approach to this crisis. Design professionals are required to make increasingly sophisticated decisions which affect a complex society. They are subject to crises of all dimensions — economic, psychological, legal. It is primarily the psychological category that this section will focus on: specifically the concept of stress and how it bears on decision-making. What causes stress? How does it interfere with normal activity? How can its effects be controlled?

To a design professional, stress is the "action on a body of any system of balanced forces whereby strain or deformation results." This is a purely technical definition, but it can be extended and easily understood as applying to human elements in the construction industry as well. In this sense, it is loosely defined as a "threat to fulfillment of basic needs."

3. Developing a Fire Drill Approach

Behavioral scientists interested in documenting stress-reaction through controlled situations exposed three groups of people to experimentally induced stress. Those in the first group were given no warning nor any previous instructions on what to do in the unusual circumstance. In the second group, as soon as the stress situation was activated, a leader appeared and pointed out appropriate behavior to guide the subjects out of the difficulty. The third group was apprised of the

What are the effects of stress on the decision-making process?

possibility of a stress situation and was shown the operations which would be required in order to resolve it. This group did not face the stress situation until it had been drilled in emergency procedures.

Behavioralists found clear patterns of behavior correlated with each technique of dealing with stress. Typically, an undirected group can be expected to break down, failing to function effectively — if at all — during the stress situation. With the appearance of a leader, performance can be somewhat improved. However, a leaderless group which knows beforehand exactly what is expected of them and what to do **if and when** an emergency situation arises, fares best in the stress situation.

> As stress and anxiety mount, the individual becomes less capable of mastery. He responds to the unfamiliar situation in terms of a more habitual, and hence easier, reaction. Anything novel is threatening and the perceived danger reduces the ability to improvise. Increased effort has to be expended in order to maintain adequate behavior in the stress situation. Thus, men who have been drilled in the precise steps to take **if** an emergency arises will automatically behave appropriately **when** an emergency arises.

A clear parallel here is the fire drill. Procedures are practiced over and over in normal conditions so that a new pattern of behavior is firmly established — so firmly that it will persist even in an emergency. Alternatives must be considered — what to do if a particular exit is blocked in one situation and who to contact if the contractor is out of reach in the other. Both the obvious and the obscure must be considered and actions for all contingencies need to be delineated.

The design professional, moreover, should devise a set of procedures to be followed by members of his firm in case any of them has a "stress attack." Decision-making under stress, which might inadvertently form the basis of a liability suit, should

Good leadership helps in cases of stress, but individual preparation and understanding are far more important

Advance preparation can reduce liability hazards from the stress situation

be postponed until principals of the firm have been consulted. The firm's most skilled negotiators, as well as those most familiar with any other people involved in the situation, should be called in. Everyone must accept the fact that people who are not under stress function considerably more efficiently and rationally than those who are.

Setting up a system of drill procedures and backup operations has additional benefits: the knowledge that is acquired during the drill is retained, and contributes to the formation of new attitudes and competence in stress situations. Furthermore, confidence in one's own ability to handle emergencies goes a long way toward preventing panic. Being able to control a trying situation immediately and automatically is the surest way to avoid multiplying crises.

4. Importance of The Earliest Learned Task

Subjects in another experiment were taught how to tie knots of increasing difficulty. They were then told to tie these knots while being subjected to a series of threats. Under these conditions, while most of the subjects were able to recall how to tie the easier knots, they were unable to tie the difficult ones when instructed to do so. It is clear that under conditions of stress, the individual responds in the manner in which he was first successful under similar circumstances.

Several hypotheses can be drawn from these data which relate to contractors and design professionals. If it is true that "increased effort has to be expended in order to maintain adequate behavior in a stress situation," then the danger in falling behind on a project schedule is in exposing oneself to compounding crises and increasing stress as the backlog mounts. Due dates set for delivery of services come as scheduled, and if the design professional finds himself at that time hopelessly buried by a desk-top full of unfinished projects, he is opening himself to a continuing source of professional liability claims.

Studies point up the need for business problem-solving as part of basic engineering training

45

Since the earlier-learned skill is performed better under stress conditions than is the more recently learned one, the ideal place to acquire stress-coping skills is in the classroom. Traditionally, schools of engineering have tended to reduce to a minimum courses not specifically dealing with technical material. It would be extremely relevant for engineering students to learn precisely what is expected of them in the business world and to become aware of liability pitfalls. Such early training makes the most lasting impression on one's memory, and thus enables one so trained to survive the disorienting effects of working under stress.

5. Defensive Avoidance

Avoiding a perceived threat is a pattern of behavior in response to stress that is of the greatest importance from a liability viewpoint. In an experiment testing several types of persuasive communication having to do with dental hygiene and preventing decay, groups of subjects were exposed to information which ranged from cartoon reminders to see a dentist regularly through tape recordings of a patient's screams during an extraction. The experimenters found that when fear was strongly aroused in the latter threatening situation, the subjects tended to ignore or minimize the importance of the communication.

> In effect, strong threat resulted in defensive avoidance of the threatening aspects of the communication, an effect that was not observed in the mild or moderate threat situation.

The same sort of defensive reaction can be noted among design professionals when stress situations occur on the job. Rather than confront a situation which is fraught with discomfort and threat, it is the nature of design professionals to avoid what might be an explosive encounter with another person. Defensive avoidance can have — indeed, has had — the most appalling legal consequences. In refusing to face the other party, the

Turning your back on the problem will not solve it

design professional sets up a void into which attorneys cheerfully rush. And once the lawyer is in the picture, the design professional finds that he is **barred** from entering into any meaningful communication with those who are now dubbed "the plaintiffs." Thus, the design professionals must force themselves to squelch their avoidance reactions no matter how contrary it is to their emotional inclinations.

In business, good fences do **not** make good neighbors!

6. When Crisis Strikes

"What should I have done? I mean, I was aware that things were going to pieces on the job. I'm no lawyer. I just didn't know what to do. If someone had helped me, maybe I could have nipped these things in the bud. I tried reporting the situation to my old insurance company, and they sent me a form asking me to check off some boxes and give them the date of the claim. There was no claim. There was one later, though, because I didn't know what to do."

The foregoing statement might be made by many design professionals in private practice today. After all, design professionals have not been trained in dispute resolution, and their experience in this regard may be limited. This usually means they are handicapped when a dispute arises (unlike the other trained parties involved in a project).

When an accusation is made against a design professional, he usually experiences one of two types of behavor (or both): anger or guilt. If his reaction is anger, the normal response is to retaliate by seeking a method of countering or injuring the party making the claim. In a crisis, then, the following advice cannot be overstated: **REMAIN CALM!** This means inwardly, outwardly, and actually. A statement by a party who contends he has been wronged should be examined

Your reaction

47

calmly and objectively. Remaining calm is far easier if the fire drill approach referred to above is practiced.

Authorities in dispute handling recommend that the accused party assume a benign attitude, but seek an understanding of the other party's position. "Please, let me have the details. I would like to make notes. I want to be sure I fully understand what you are saying. Let me get this straight. You feel that the plans were lacking in what regard?" This is a far better response than a quick and heated denial.

Crisis Situation Rule No. 1: Remain calm.

You are innnocent until proven guilty

The second possible reaction by the design professional to an accusation is guilt. We are appalled at the number of claims we have been involved in where the design professional has assumed full responsibility when something unexpected occurred. Yet a more thorough examination at a later date proved this responsibility wholly erroneous since the fault lay elsewhere. It is almost impossible to undo the wrong that can be done by a party who has mistakenly assumed responsibility and communicated it to other parties connected with a loss. The acceptance of blame is so prevalent, however, that it is given a name: The Good Guy Syndrome. It is a way of saying that design professionals strive to perform with such skill and competence that **nothing** can go wrong. This is impossible. But their sense of identity with the project on which they have worked may be so strong they are willing to accept fault even when it is not theirs.

Crisis Situation Rule No. 2: No matter what the facts appear to be, do not immediately assume that you are responsible.

Although you should not assume responsibility, neither should you fail to communicate with others. In short, keep talking. Do not withdraw into a shell.

Crisis Situation Rule No. 3: Communicate.

While the first three admonitions for handling a crisis situation are correct in theory, it must be remembered that despite the best of intentions to remain calm and free of guilt, trouble usually causes emotional stress. As explained earlier, a person's ability to cope with a situation is greatly diminished by emotional involvement. Then, too, there is a great likelihood that he is not an expert at crisis resolution.

Mankind has developed techniques for coping with crises. Fire departments, police departments, Coast Guard, rescue squads, etc. are groups trained for many types of emergencies. What the design professional in private practice needs is a squad of experts trained in professional liability crises with the knowledge and ability needed to resolve the crises in the most efficient and expert manner.

Seek help early

When should the design professional call on this "Fire Department"? The answer is not easy. He should seek outside help long before an actual claim is made. In fact, he should seek aid immediately if he senses that a situation is developing into a claim. He should not wait until things have developed to such a state that negotiations are impossible, or that special strategies are useless. This does not mean that he should turn for help on every simple matter which becomes a dispute. But if he perceives that a possible claim may ensue, he should call his insurer and his legal counsel.

Crisis Situation Rule No. 4: Call in outside help when it is felt that there is an impending threat which might give rise to a professional liability claim.

Document facts

In any combative situation, preparedness is a key word, particularly if faced with a possible courtroom battle. Therefore, the next step in a crisis situation would be the preparation of a file. All data relating to the work should be clarified. Notes concerning duties and the responsibilities of the various parties should be lucid and kept current. Detailed notes should be kept on any communications with other parties. **Never rely on recall.**

All correspondence must be reviewed. Those items contained in the file that relate to the dispute must be marked and their content noted. The plans and specifications, and the contract document, should be reviewed. Those sections which refer to the problem or which specify the duties of the parties involved in the dispute should be noted. If a product is involved, the manufacturer's or supplier's specifications should be obtained. If shop drawings are involved, those which pertain to the claim should be examined and the application noted.

Notes and records of all types not only help clarify the status of a crisis, but they provide ammunition for a defense counsel or dispute consultant who may come to your rescue. Thus, preparedness in this case means thorough documentation.

Closely related to the previous recommendation is another form of documentation: photography. "A good picture is worth a thousand words," may sound trite, yet it continues to be good advice in potential professional liability claims situations. Photographing the disputed subject matter **thoroughly** is an excellent way of preserving the record for the future. Memories dim. A photographic record could later prove invaluable.

Crisis Situation Rule No. 5: Document and photograph.

Remaining flexible and seeking solutions to a crisis before it escalates into a major lawsuit should be an obvious rule. Unfortunately, as adversary positions are taken, it is a rule sometimes overlooked.

Crisis Situation Rule No. 6: Seek alternatives.

By following the above rules, chances are good that a design professional will clearly outline the problem — frequently absolving his firm completely. In some instances, responsibilities for failure may overlap several parties. In such cases conflict resolution techniques, outlined below, should be used. When self-coordination fails, outside mediators should sometimes be invited to evaluate the degree of responsiblity. Only as a last resort should litigation be considered.

Coordinate then mediate

Crisis Situation Rule No. 7: Seek to resolve the conflict in coordination with others involved. If self-coordination fails, seek mediation.

7. When Litigation Becomes Inevitable

Exhibits 3 and 4 graphically represent the nightmare of professional liability claims and the accompanying litigation. This is one of the most traumatic and enervating experiences a design professional in private practice may have. The entire litigation process is not only formidable, but a monumental waste of time and money as well.

Wasted time and money

Consider the pain and agony that goes with each of the steps shown:

- Being served the summons and complaint;

- Consulting with your attorney;

- Notifying your insurance carrier;

- Holding conferences to determine the relationship of the parties;

- Determining whether insurance coverage is in effect;

- Analyzing the plans and specifications, and exhaustively researching detail;

- Filing an answer and cross complaint; and,

- Experiencing the trauma of a courtroom battle.

There is usually an average of three to five years of charge and countercharge, depositions, interrogatories, and testimonies before trial. The final decision is then left in the hands of a jury, people who are unskilled in the practices of modern day construction. Idiotic? It would seem so. Thus, it is well in order to take the time to learn to resolve crises before they become claims. Keep this in mind the next time you are in a job dispute which appears to be getting out of hand.

An ounce of loss prevention is worth a pound of courtroom cure

EXHIBIT 3

ANATOMY OF A CONFLICT

Rules for Conflict Mitigation

- remain calm
- do not assume responsibility, no matter what your immediate conclusion
- maintain your lines of communication with all parties
- call in outside expert advice (crisis event "firemen")
- ascertain the facts, document everything
- photograph when possible
- utilize conflict resolution techniques to coordinate differences
- if dispute becomes stalemated, seek mediation
- use litigation as a last resort

EXHIBIT 4
TYPICAL LITIGATION SEQUENCE

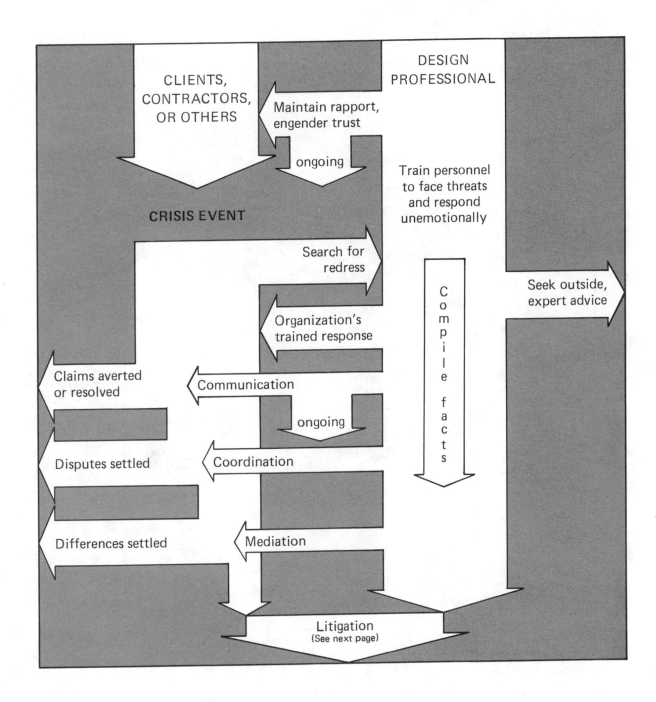

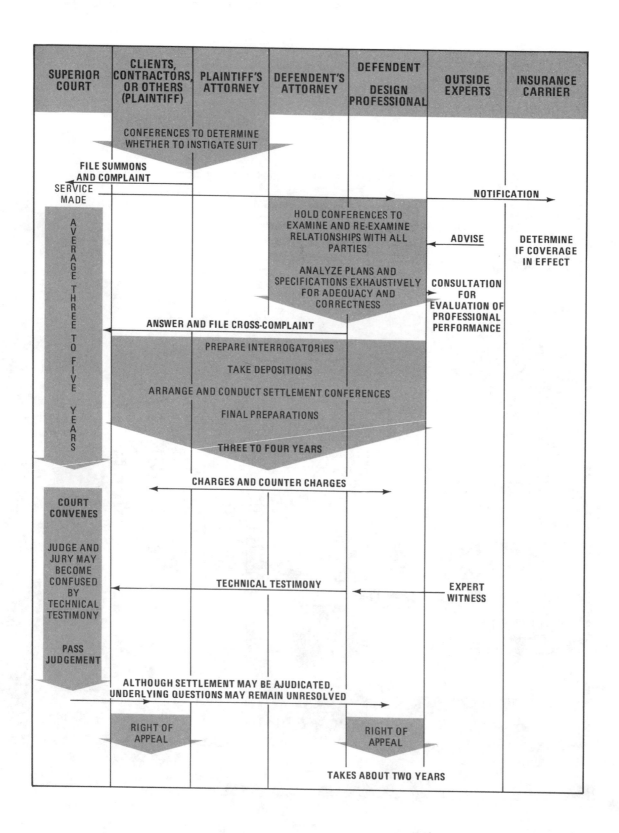

SUPERIOR COURT	CLIENTS, CONTRACTORS, OR OTHERS (PLAINTIFF)	PLAINTIFF'S ATTORNEY	DEFENDENT'S ATTORNEY	DEFENDENT DESIGN PROFESSIONAL	OUTSIDE EXPERTS	INSURANCE CARRIER

CONFERENCES TO DETERMINE WHETHER TO INSTIGATE SUIT

FILE SUMMONS AND COMPLAINT

SERVICE MADE

NOTIFICATION

AVERAGE THREE TO FIVE YEARS

HOLD CONFERENCES TO EXAMINE AND RE-EXAMINE RELATIONSHIPS WITH ALL PARTIES

ADVISE

DETERMINE IF COVERAGE IN EFFECT

ANALYZE PLANS AND SPECIFICATIONS EXHAUSTIVELY FOR ADEQUACY AND CORRECTNESS

CONSULTATION FOR EVALUATION OF PROFESSIONAL PERFORMANCE

ANSWER AND FILE CROSS-COMPLAINT

PREPARE INTERROGATORIES

TAKE DEPOSITIONS

ARRANGE AND CONDUCT SETTLEMENT CONFERENCES

FINAL PREPARATIONS

THREE TO FOUR YEARS

CHARGES AND COUNTER CHARGES

COURT CONVENES

JUDGE AND JURY MAY BECOME CONFUSED BY TECHNICAL TESTIMONY

TECHNICAL TESTIMONY

EXPERT WITNESS

PASS JUDGEMENT

ALTHOUGH SETTLEMENT MAY BE AJUDICATED, UNDERLYING QUESTIONS MAY REMAIN UNRESOLVED

RIGHT OF APPEAL

RIGHT OF APPEAL

TAKES ABOUT TWO YEARS

8. The Relevance of Human Relations

Recall the opening scene — two emotionally charged men are coming together. A hostile, disruptive exchange is inevitable — or is it? What if the contractor and the design professional had worked together on several jobs in the past? What if they liked working together? Would this past history change the outcome of their meeting? Common sense as well as research findings of social scientists testify that it would. Bonds of loyalty and cooperation built up over time do not dissolve during a crisis; in fact, successful resolution of difficult situations tends to cement these bonds. The formation of loyalty bonds can be established even over a short period of time. We are most loyal to, and appreciative of, those people who increase our self-esteem rather than threaten it, as the following example illustrates.

Almost accidental circumstances caused the assignment of a heating contractor's best men to a small job instead of the personnel who ordinarily would have done it. The work went smoothly with admirable coordination among all parties. Craftsmanship was excellent, and none of the usual problems arose during the project or after its completion. The design professional, expecting the customary barely acceptable performance for a small job, was so startled and pleased with the outcome that he wrote a complimentary letter to the heating contractor.

The contractor wrote back that it was the first time in his thirty years in business that any design professional had written such a letter. He promised to — and did — exert extra effort in all future work for that design professional.

This example, describing the experience of two individuals can be extrapolated to the entire profession. In every project, two individuals make the basic agreement; their relationship can set the frame of mind for every worker involved on that project; genuine care and personal thanks are extremely effective techniques of loss prevention in this impersonal age of mass production. Furthermore, they stress the crucial human element

Courtesy, mutual respect, friendship all contribute to avoiding legal problems

which is all too often dismissed as "nonessential to the project."

It is good human relations — and better business practice — to develop in others a sense of pride in their work. Watch for good work; express recognition and appreciation when you find it.

9. Summary

What is stress? What are its effects? What can be done about it?

Stress is a threat to the fulfillment of basic human needs. When under stress, one's ability to handle the more complex and recently learned patterns of behavior is substantially reduced. The number of professional liability cases which can be traced to decisions made by an individual under stress is staggering.

Some simple but effective steps can be taken

To cope successfully with stress, the design professional must recognize that threatening situations are inevitable, and that his most natural response —defensive avoidance — is his greatest danger.

Four precepts to keep in mind:

a. The Drill Approach

Analyze all the potential emergencies that may arise. Plan a method of dealing with each contingency. Drill all personnel thoroughly, so that if a difficulty arises, they will deal with it automatically without hesitation.

b. The Back-Up Team

When any member of your firm is enmeshed in a stress situation, advise a principal immediately, and arrange for your most skilled negotiators to come into the situation.

c. Overcome the Avoidance Syndrome

Repress the natural instinct to avoid unpleasant encounters. Remember that when irate participants refuse to iron out problems, only their lawyers can prosper.

d. Interpersonal Relations

Establish good interpersonal relationships with clients, contractors and all potential claimants. Good human relations make for the best business relations.

E. Modern Theories of Conflict Resolution

Conflict is a natural state

Conflicts and their resolution are such common occurrences in our daily interpersonal and organizational relationships that they are seldom confronted on a conscious level. Let us consider their frequency in our daily lives.

Conflict can and does arise at home from friction with spouses or children; from occasional unpleasant contacts with public personnel or authorities; in business, from such frustrations as delay in arrival of anxiously awaited equipment; or in day-to-day dealings with employees, supervisors, and with professionals in other disciplines.

Fortunately, personal conflicts are usually resolved without the intervention of marriage counselors, policemen, or outside arbitrators. Resolutions of organizational conflicts, on the other hand, are achieved all too frequently after indulgence by the protagonists in spirited games of strategy and counterstrategy.

Conflict will flare occasionally to a point requiring experts or arbitrators to conduct the action leading to resolution. This has been described by behavioralists studying conflict as a state of limited war. In limited war, the experts take over the conflict situation.

For the design professional embroiled in legal conflict, the battlefield is the courtroom, the weapons are arguments, and the evidence is presented by generals in the persons of attorneys. There is no question that in this highly programmed arena, with its formality and ritual, control of resolution of the conflict is no longer in the possession of the original participants. It is expedient, therefore, to achieve resolution before the state of limited war is reached.

An individual's attitude toward conflict depends on what he unconsciously takes for granted, according to one expert. Again, most often it is what we do not know about an event or condition (hidden issues) that results in conflict which will do us harm. It follows, then, that an approach to solution of a conflict should be preceded by a critical appraisal of our own personal attitude toward it, and an examination of **all** circumstances surrounding it.

Learning to cope with conflict

1. What is Conflict?

    In order to cope effectively with conflict, we must define it. Further, the influence and conditions which may be identified with successful resolution of conflict need to be set forth. One theory of conflict gives a tangible definition of its components upon which there may be based some concrete action to control its outcome. Game theory, as it is popularly called, reduces social behavior to strategies which provide the opportunity to examine conflict in the context of a game.

    Conflict may be defined as a competitive event. The parties are moved to action when loss is anticipated. They see their positions as being incompatible, requiring action to avoid adverse effects. Consider the following example, which we shall later refer to as the "excavation extra" conference.

    An excavation contractor encounters unexpected subsurface conditions. He anticipates the need for an expensive extra to complete the work and communicates the fact to the design professional who, in turn, reports the need to the owner. The owner calls in the soil and foundation engineer. A meeting is arranged.

The stage for conflict is set if each party sees himself as potentially responsible for the additional cost.

In the "excavation extra" conference, each party aspires to a resolution goal. As long as each party desires a condition or position that is contrary to those of the others, there will be attempts to dominate or triumph to the detriment of the others.

2. Selection of Strategy

The study of conflict in the game context has led to the conclusion that, to obtain goals, the control and resoluton of conflict depend upon recognizing and acting upon the factors affecting the resolution process. It would be convenient if rules and conventions could be established for conflicts such as those we observe in chess and bridge. However, each party brings to the conflict varying attitudes relating to professional responsibility, to opinions as to legal obligations, to his own competence, etc.

These attitudes are sometimes more overpowering than monetary considerations. All the factors bear upon the course and outcome of conflict resolution.

Attitudes are sometimes more powerful than money

Evidence of these variable factors can be seen in those professional liability lawsuits that involve relatively minor sums for alleged damages. In one instance, a design professional was advised by parties to the construction project that they felt he had a certain obligation for damages which occurred after the start-up of a system. Damages amounted to something less than $2,500. There was no question in the design professional's mind that the loss was clearly attributable to the contractor and a representative of the municipality. He therefore advised all parties to the conflict that it would be up to the others to determine responsibility. Copies of further written information were received, noted, and filed. A summons and complaint, naming the design professional as well as the other parties, was served upon him after the passage of some two or three months. Clearly, monetary considerations alone did not trigger the escalation of this conflict into a lawsuit.

Three possible ways to resolve a conflict

The outcome of any conflict is highly dependent upon how well all parties understand and coordinate their actions. It has been found in conflict situations that a decision to select the most favorable outcome for one can result in excessively detrimental results for others. Under the same circumstances, a decision to select a less favorable outcome by one party may result in a positive outcome for all. This leads us to consider the three possible choices which may affect the final result.

First, a party may decide to maximize his own outcome. **Assume in the "excavation extra" conference that the owner decides upon this course of action. He makes a statement to the effect that one or all of the others at the conference will have to decide how to absorb the unexpected extra expense.**

The second choice is the decision to minimize another's outcome. **To exemplify this, the design professional assumes a position that supports the owner, thereby minimizing the stance of the contractor.**

The third and last possible choice is an effort to maximize the combined outcome of all parties to the conflict. **This choice would be best illustrated in the "excavation extra" conference by the design professional stating at the outset that the purpose of the conference is to explore possible actions which may lead to reduction of the anticipated extra costs, or at least to make an initial effort**

to minimize conflict, and that sharing responsibility represents a minor expense as compared to the cost of out-of-hand conflict.

Before considering the influences which must be recognized as implementing effective coordination of strategies (or motives), let us consider two environments in which conflict and its resolution may be conducted. They are a) threat and b) trust.

3. Conflict Environment — Threat

There is a great temptaton to use threat in reaching resolutions, not only because it seems easier, but because it is an instinctive human reaction that has existed since man inhabited caves. Further, as we shall see later, much less effort is required in the use of mutual threat and retaliation than in the conscious effort required in developing mutual trust. When no other avenue remains open, threat then may be the only possible alternative available for the resolution of certain conflicts.

The primary consideration in the effective use of threat is credibility. Threat is a warning of the commission of some act which will be costly to all participants. **In the "excavation extra" conference, the threat of a lawsuit is most convincingly conveyed by evidence that legal counsel has recommended such an action.**

In the threat environment, it is wise to pose threats in steps which may be executed individually. To carry out a threat on this basis reinforces credibility. It also prevents escalation to a point where court action is inevitable. Conflict easily deepens and tends to be impossible to resolve without severe negative consequences for all in the threat environment.

4. Conflict Environment — Trust

The atmosphere most conducive to maximizing the outcome for all parties to conflict is one in

Threat — the easiest, instinctive reaction

which mutual trust is established. Rules for the application of this powerful principle are relatively straightforward.

To begin with, trust requires that at least one person puts himself on the line and risks something. **In our "excavation extra" conference this would be exemplified by a proposal from the design professional to consider any design alternative that would reduce the cost of the "excavation extra."** Thus, application of the trust principle is strongest when one player leaves himself open to attack; in effect, he is risking defeat.

The whole process of building trust demands unbiased communication. This is accomplished by the mutual acknowledgement of rationality and good intentions.

5. Role-Playing Technique

Each participant must place himself in the other party's position. This technique — role-playing — is widely used by psychiatrists, family counselors, social psychologists, and debate coaches — persons who have an interest in making sure that both sides of an issue are fairly seen. One of two things is accomplished by role-playing. First, it may be discovered that another party is right. Secondly, although the other party may be wrong, the goal of convincing him that you understand his position has been attained.

Role-playing itself requires a dialogue in which the opponent is given the opportunity to ascertain that his position is clearly understood, and he must acknowledge the correctness of the understanding of his position.

In the "excavation extra" conference, assume that the contractor feels that all or part of the extra cost should be borne by the soil and foundation engineer. The contractor's expressed position must then be restated by the other participants. The dia-

logue will end when the contractor is satisfied with the restatement.

6. Factors Facilitating Cooperation

In developing trust, and hence cooperation, one needs valid points of a position. To do anything else at this point works only to the detriment of the buildup of trust. Trust environment is achieved when all participants join in the role-playing activity, to establish a basis of common agreement. **In our conference, then, at this point an effort should be made by the soil engineer to induce the contractor to go through the same role-playing process himself.**

Studies have indicated that trust and cooperation are at a maximum when four points have been communicated:

Four points for maximizing trust

- Expectation: What the parties are expected to do.
- Intention: What the participants intend to do or would like to do.
- Retaliation: What the participants will do if they are not successful in gaining cooperation.
- Resolution: Suggestions as to what is necessary to correct the situation.

7. Factors Inhibiting Cooperation

There are dynamic influences that inhibit cooperation, coordination of strategy, or the establishment of a mutual motive. First, parties in a conflict situation who are aware that their relationship will be of brief duration are more likely to resist mutual coordination of motives. **In the "excavation extra" conference, assume the contractor is working outside his normal area of operations. He has not worked with this construction team in the past. Further, it can be reasonably anticipated that he will not be working with them in the future. Un-**

Length of working relationship

der these conditions, every party may elect strategies to maximize his own position. Regardless of the other factors bearing upon this particular conference, there is a likelihood that the excavation contractor will be asked to bear the brunt of the resolution.

On the other hand, if all parties to the conflict have had, and do anticipate, a longer term of relationship, cooperation between them is more probable, if only because of fear that the tables may be turned in the course of some future interaction.

Communication

A second influence upon cooperation or coordination of motives is communication. Its importance has already been pointed out in the development of trust. A beneficial exchange of pure information occurs as well as an increased knowledge about the expectations of others in the course of communication. **In the "excavation extra" conference, it is possible that some of those invited may fail to attend the conference because they have confidence in the ability of the others to come to a satisfactory coordination of effort leading to resolution. This could occur; however, resolution is much more likely to happen if there is active communication among all parties.**

Ignorance

A third influence, ignorance on the part of one or more of the conflict contestants can, and unfortunately does, lead to deterioration of efforts toward coordination. **If the excavation contractor in the "excavation extra" conference is not qualified for the project, all may find themselves embroiled in a conflict which may be difficult — if not impossible — to resolve.** It is too often assumed that the requisite knowledge and understanding of the circumstances is possessed by all. Recognize ignorance, therefore, as a definite negative influence in obtaining coordination of strategies.

Group support

A fourth influence upon cooperation is the individual organization or group support behind the individual participants. There is considerable evidence for the proposition of some theorists that there would never be conflict without groups or organizations. **In the "excavation extra" conference, as in any other conflict situation, an effort must be made to determine the influence the individual organizations have upon their participating representatives. Personnel who are instructed to act co-operatively perform better in strategy coordination efforts than those who are told to maximize their own organization's position. If our owner's representative is under instructions to maximize his position — that is, to bear as little, if any, of the extra cost as possible — efforts at coordination will be hindered.** Recognize this influence of the individual organization. It is sometimes possible to change an organization's attitude.

The final factor for consideration bearing upon coordination of strategies, or motives, is the presence of an accommodating party to the conflict. This type of individual offers solutions which require no concessions by other parties. **In the course of the "excavation extra" conference, the soil and foundation engineer makes an offer to absorb ten percent of the additional cost. The offer is made without requirements or commitments on the part of the others as to which of them will bear the remainder of the exposure.** This accommodating action often invites the opposite of what is intended — competitiveness. One may naturally expect efforts, at this point, to take advantage of the party making the accommodating offer. Recognize that unilateral accommodations do not aid in the co-operation. Rather they may lead to an escalation of conflict.

Accommodating party

8. Conflict Resolution and Professional Liability

It is acknowledged that escalated conflict resulting in professional liability lawsuits occurs because of hidden or unsuspected issues.

In developing conflict resolution skills, the design professional arms himself with a powerful new tool to alleviate the ravaging effects of a professional liability lawsuit. Many have followed the avenue of defensive avoidance, i.e. avoiding a conflict situation by refusing to participate. This course is wrong. It is increasingly clear that unattended conflict situations grow like a virulent disease to plague those who had hoped to be spared. Early detection and efforts to control conflict, like preventative medicine, can spare untold agony. In the complex systems in which the design professional is involved, he is almost always operating in an environment with many other individuals and organizations. Conflict is inevitable. Acknowledging its inevitability leads us to search out methods to control it and to prevent the destruction of reputations, business relationships, and the financial stability of those who are involved.

Commence by confronting conflict. Take an approach which may be stated as follows:

- Make every effort to maximize the combined outcome of a conflict, to the benefit of all parties.

- Encourage efforts to create an atmosphere of trust.

- Avoid the influences which may interfere with the goal of maximizing the outcome for all concerned.

This approach is most easily achieved by early efforts to resolve conflict. Remember that early resolution of conflict will provide the design professional with reinforced protection against the expense of professional liability lawsuits. Above all other considerations, keep in mind that over half of the costs of all settlements that go to litigation end in the pockets of the plaintiff and defense attorneys.

F. Dealing With Human Frailties

A design professional in the western part of the United States was asked recently to name the most difficult task he faced in his practice. He avowed it was explaining to a client why certain human errors were made which had resulted in a delay or extra cost, but which could have been avoided. Total absence of mistakes is, of course, impossible. Regardless of this truth, clients who are willing to accept this explanation without protest are rare.

Design professionals report that the types of human errors which create claims frequently involve memory, judgment, capability, schedules, and habits. Although our human frailties are exhibited in many other ways, these categories represent the basis for a substantial number of problems that lead to claims against design professionals. Other businesses and professions have devised methods to reduce the incidence of claims from these sources. These same remedies can be modified and adapted by the design professional.

1. Memory

How do people remember and why do they forget? Although we have relatively little knowledge about the function of memory, there are a few principles which psychologists have discovered. Basically, they have found that when a person claims to have forgotten something, usually he has not really learned it in the first place. Therefore, to analyze why people forget is to examine the ways in which people learn.

For learning to take place, the individual must be attentive and motivated to learn. Take the situation of two persons introduced at a cocktail party. The very hasty "Mr. Jones, this is Mr. Smith" will not be remembered unless one of the parties makes a point to learn the other's name. Memory experts suggest that a person associate names with some characteristic of the persons he meets. A Mr. Brown might be associated with the person's brown hair or eyes or even his physique

Memory involves association and repetition

(i.e., the word brawn sounds like brown). The more times information is repeated, the more probable that it will be committed to memory. Therefore, another often used memory tool is to repeat the name a few times in the course of a conversation. These two principles, association and repetition, are basic to the processes of learning and remembering. Association and repetition can be utilized in the business world as well as in social situations, for both oral and written communications.

The design professional, as a student, practiced the principles of association and repetition daily in his studies until effective remembering became a habit. However, for the practitioner who has been away from a classroom for many years, this habit has often been discarded. As a student, he would never dream of attending a lecture without his notebook, nor expect to pass a course without reviewing his notes, committing them to memory, and questioning those areas he did not clearly understand. Yet later, in his daily work routine as a design professional he leaves these habits behind. He often expects to remember the details of important telephone discussions or conferences concerning an active project without the help of notes or other memory tools. Yet, it is even more critical for the design professional to use memory tools than for the student. Memory failure or incomplete understanding on the part of the practicing design professional can cost him huge sums of money and precious time if litigation occurs.

One simple way for the design professional to reduce these risks is to record all telephone discussions which in any way concern or influence a project. There are two important advantages he can gain by this procedure.

a. In the event of litigation, a dated memorandum (such as shown in Exhibit 1) which briefly describes the discussion, can be extremely valuable as evidence. In many jurisdictions, this type of memorandum may be admitted as

Memory lapses cured by telephone and conversation logs

evidence of a past event recorded or used to refresh the memory of a witness.

b. A telephone log of conversations during the course of a design serves as an excellent means of following the progress of the project.

Such memoranda and logs (see Exhibit 5) are particularly useful if for some reason the principal project professional cannot continue (becomes ill, leaves the firm, or is transferred to another project), and another professional unfamiliar with the project is required to take over and complete the work.

2. Judgment

No two design professionals, presented with the same design problem, will produce identical solutions. Although the design of both may be complete in all respects, the drawings carefully drafted, and the specifications unambiguous, distinct differences between the two may exist from the professional liability standpoint. One design may create far more controversy in the form of claims. Something more basic than a difference in the competence of contractors lies at the base of this problem. To a great extent, design judgment, or the lack of it, determines the degree of difficulty encountered on a project.

Sound design judgment can determine the degree of difficulty encountered on a project

Do certain professional personnel in your office have a talent for making better design judgments than others? Aside from mathematical accuracy, do some have a better overall sense of proportion in a given design situation than others? If so, is this a natural talent or can this quality be fostered among those who may be presently lacking it?

First, consider what constitutes good design judgment. It is sometimes defined as that quality which enables the evaluation of alternative choices and selection of an optimum solution to a design problem — not only from a purely artistic or technical point of view, but from a consideration of the practical aspects as well.

What constitutes sound design judgment

EXHIBIT 5

TELEPHONE CONVERSATION RECORD
P. D. & Q., Inc.

Project # : 6872

Client: JOHN DOE, ARCHITECT

Project: VERY TALL OFFICE BLDG.

Location: ILLINOIS CITY

Date/Time	Call From	Call To	Discussion
4/6/79 10:30 A.M.	JOHN DOE	RICH ROE	1. The main mechanical equip. rm. must be reloc. from S.W. corner to S.E. corner on same level, (per JOHN DOE).
4/6/79 1:40 P.M.	RICH ROE	JOHN DOE	1. The relocated mech. equip. rm. is to be changed in dimensions to accommodate Scheme 1-A layout. Our Scheme 2-A was rejected by John Doe because it created restricted areas adjacent to mech. equip. room.

Extensive academic training and a wide range of practical experience play a great part in the acquisition of sound design judgment. For those practitioners who lack superior training and experience, however, short courses and assignment to specially selected projects may partially fill their deficiencies. The most obvious short-range measure is to require that relatively inexperienced project people be tutored in their decisions by other, more experienced personnel. Holding frequent progress reviews on those projects handled by less experienced personnel also is beneficial.

As a long-range measure, emphasize your desire for higher quality judgments. Designated principals should make an increased effort to record examples of a particular individual's judgmental errors. There are some designers who possess the innate ability to make good design judgments but are unaware of its immense value. Such a person can frequently progress from the status of a satisfactory employee to that of a highly valuable member of your staff by the use of frequent instruction couched in terms which leave no doubt in his mind of your confidence in his ultimate improvement. Enhancement of your professional workforce can be facilitated if you establish a rating system for each of your project professionals. Each should be made aware of your high regard for sound design judgment. Carefully note any improvement in your more error-prone designers and express your appreciation of their progress.

III
business
procedures

III
business
procedures

A. The Design Professional As A Businessman

Most design professionals enter practice ill-equipped to cope with the myriad of business requirements (payrolls, taxes, business licensing, etc.). Technical schools rarely require any education in these areas and professional licensing agencies do not test a design professional's proficiency in day-to-day business procedures. Hence it is not surprising to discover that the lack of knowledge, or acquisition of only minimal knowledge in business procedures, has had a marked effect on exposure to claims.

When design professionals deal with other design professionals or when businessmen deal with other businessmen, the parties operate on a relative par with one another; no one is placed at an inherent disadvantage. But when the design professional deals with businessmen concerning **business** problems, the design professional almost always finds himself handicapped. Learning to play the other man's game on nearly equal terms has become not only advisable but essential to his self-preservation.

If you agree that this step is necessary, much can be learned from the world of commerce. For example, before any sale, a knowledgeable businessman always makes an evaluation of the financial capabilities of his customers, even if only in a rudimentary fashion. In constrast, few design professionals question their client's reputation for prompt payment of fees or their capacity to finance a project adequately. One way to evaluate a client and a project before finalizing the negotiations is to use a Project Evaluator, exemplified in Exhibit 6.

Learning from the world of commerce

Rare is the businessman who offers a product or service for sale and does not reduce an agreement to writing. Yet there are design professionals who complete major design projects on the basis of a preliminary negotiation, a telephone call, or a brief conversation with a client.

Personnel policies and hiring practices among businessmen are, almost without exception, extremely well-defined. Yet many design professionals depend upon their first impression and subjective appraisal when hiring new employees; they see no value in having well thought out company hiring policies in writing.

Examine your own procedures. In your practice do you utilize the most modern, sophisticated and successful techniques in performing your technical services and yet retain roll-top desk business practices? If so, immediate measures are required to correct this situation. To survive in our present lawsuit-happy society you must exercise at least the same degree of care in your **business** procedures as you do in the technical aspects of your practice. By establishing consistent professional level quality in both aspects of your practice, you will effectively cut the likelihood of accusations of professional incompetence.

B. The Money Trap

Under present conditions, we may well expect to find on the design profession's headstone an epitaph

EXHIBIT 6

PROJECT EVALUATOR

PROJECT: _____

OWNER: _____ CLIENT: _____

LOCATION: _____ DATE: _____

Place an X below the correct answer

		YES	UNKNOWN	NO
1.	Have we dealt with the client before?			
2.	Do we have personal knowledge of the owner's financial stability and his general reputation?			
3.	Does the client pay his bills promptly?			
4.	Is the project, particularly our portion of the work, properly funded?			
5.	Is the project of the type that we have worked on before both successfully and frequently?			
6.	Are we sure our work load will not be strained by taking on this project at this time?			
7.	Is the project within easy traveling distance of our office (one of our offices)?			
8.	Will the time schedule for completion of our portion of the work be easy to comply with?			
9.	Is the contract with the client equitable?			
10.	Are labor conditions in the area where work is to be performed calm?			
11.	Is the contract free of hold harmless and indemnity provisions?			
12.	Is the contractor (or contractors) who will probably perform the work personally known to us to be capable and competent?			
13.	Is the project free of speculative aspects?			
14.	Does the design we will use have wide acceptance in our discipline?			
15.	Will our fee be wholly adequate?			
16.	Are we to perform review of the construction to see that it is implemented in accordance with the plans and specifications?			
17.	Is our crew used to this type of project?			
18.	Are the Code requirements routine?			
19.	Is the Owner providing funds for unexpected contingencies?			
20.	Will we be proud to have our firm's name associated with this project?			
21.	Have we checked the insurance requirements and found there are no special insurance needs?			
22.	Our agreement is not as a joint venture on this project?			
23.	Will our firm make a fair profit by taking this job?			
24.	Will we have the opportunity of reviewing the bids and making recommendations to the owner before contract is let?			
25.	Will the budget make it easy to design and remain within the budget figure?			

If you have more than five X's in the no column or five in the unknown column, think twice about accepting the work.

which states:

> The Design Professionals,
> We grieve their demise,
> Projects short of money
> They could not recognize.

From this somewhat macabre prediction we can elicit a principle: View with trepidation any project which gives evidence of a lack of sufficient financing.

Now transform this maxim into your everyday business practice:

Is your client broke?

1. Routinely check the financial stability of each client for every project before you agree to commit your services.

2. Routinely advise every client to maintain a reserve of funds throughout the course of the construction to meet any unexpected needs which may arise.

3. Routinely refuse work, at least until further investigation, when approached by a client who appears to want top-quality professional services but whose conduct arouses your suspicion that sufficient funds may not be available to do an adequate job.

An astonishing number of claims against design professionals can be traced, at least in part, to the fact that the owner or the contractor did not allocate sufficient capital to do the necessary work. It would seem that such a problem should concern only the owner, contractor, and related financing institutions. However, when the dollar squeeze begins, you may find yourself vulnerable to a desperate owner or contractor caught midway in construction of the project and grasping for solutions and money.

Consider a predicament. Deliberately, or perhaps by inadvertence, the owner and contractor have committed themselves and their resources to the completion of the project. Now the owner discovers to his dismay that the costs are rapidly mounting far beyond anything he contemplated. The slightest delay or unanticipated expense magnifies his dilemma. His reaction is quite natural and predictable. He begins to strike out in all directions to maintain some degree of stability and fend off impending disaster. The contractor is similarly threatened but has a relatively superior bargaining position compared to the design professional. He has the advantage of being in a position where the owner must seek to induce him to complete performance. The design professional's principal function has been completed, however, and he may await only the completion of the project to collect the remainder of his fee.

Are you low man on a totem pole?

With this scenario, who can be expected to bear the brunt of an exasperated and harassed owner or contractor? You, the design professional, of course. The slightest ambiguity in the contract documents which coincides with the contractor's request for extra payment is made to order for a claim against you. The natural reaction of an unsympathetic owner is to claim that the cost of any extra work and consequential delays are solely attributable to your negligence in not providing sufficiently clear drawings and specifications. The fact that such a claim is eventually found to be without merit is of little consolation when you consider the hidden expenses that are not reimbursable, such as prospective clients lost due to adverse publicity, the time lost preparing for possible litigation, and the litigation if it ensues.

Picking and choosing clients and jobs

In a nutshell, you should recognize that **client selection, contractor selection** and **project selection** are just as important, if not more so, as the system selection or material and equipment selection.

One claims situation related to this problem area is illustrated by the **Guess What is Behind the Wall** type of project. One design professional in a small city was asked to compile a report indicating the extent of air conditioning modifications required for an old building to which a new addition was being attached. The design professional was not able to locate reliable as-built drawings showing the extent of the original system. Exploratory demolition was considered too expensive by the owner and the design professional was requested to base his recommendations upon a visual inspection only. Later, the system components, ductwork and piping were exposed and discovered to be in poor condition and inadequate for the new design. The design professional made supplemental recommendations which necessitated additional and costly modifications. The owner had chosen to use the design professional's original report as the basis for an agreement with the contractor. The owner accepted the design professional's supplemental recommendations as necessary extra work but because the design professional had not furnished this information in his original report, the owner sued for the additional cost. Circuitous reasoning? Perhaps so. But nevertheless the design professional was in trouble.

What went wrong? The design professional acted in a perfectly reasonable, ethical, and professional manner; perhaps it could be argued that the owner did not. If we look behind the entire transaction at matters within the design professional's control, we can observe two mistakes, neither of which may constitute professional negligence, but which are nonetheless reasons for generating this type of claim.

Can you do it for me wholesale?

First, the design professional selected the wrong type of client. When he was informed by the owner that insufficient funds were available to conduct exploratory demolition to determine the condition and extent of the existing system, he should have recognized this as a danger signal indicating a possible claims situation.

Second, the design professional would have acted more prudently had he included in the report a precautionary statement that no design or construction budget should be based on this preliminary information and that additional cost might well be necessary after complete information was obtained.

The principle to be extracted is quite simple but of immense importance to your professional well-being — projects with inadequate funding frequently lead to professional liability claims against the design professionals.

When a prospective client attempts to induce you to work for a fee you consider inadequate, you should be prepared to refuse. The manner in which you refuse, however, can influence him to change his mind. Give him the benefit of the doubt; his attitude concerning your fee may have been adopted because of insufficient information. Rather than resent his actions you should attempt to apprise him of the fact that a reduction in professional fees may actually result in a higher cost of construction.

One design professional sends a friendly, informative letter which presents a viewpoint often overlooked by clients. The pertinent portions of the letter are as follows:

> Thank you for giving us the opportunity to provide design services for your project. From your description of it, we are sure we would enjoy working on it. The magnitude and degree of complexity of your project, however, would require more design effort than we could afford to schedule at the fee you suggest. Your financial budget, we are sure, has been carefully assembled and we know you have a responsibility to keep the cost of the project within certain limits. Our past experience shows, however, that sometimes one point is overlooked; that is, the cost of a project will in part be determined by the competence of the professionals who design it. In fact, the **total** cost of a project (including the design fee), may often be reduced by more thorough planning, investigation of materials and construction review. If you have inadvertently omitted this consideration from your budget study, we are sure you will not resent our calling it to your attention. It is a factor easily overlooked and could save you money in the long run.

> If you agree, perhaps we can discuss the project further. We plan to call you in a few days and if you have any questions we will be happy to answer them. We look forward to further discussions with you and your staff.

You get what you pay for

Although we do not recommend your untailored use of this exact wording, it demonstrates one design professional's response to a common problem. The results of this approach can be much more rewarding than if you were to issue a brusque rejection or, even worse, to accept the project for a fee which is wholly inadequate.

C. Capabilities

Can do?

Some design professional firms, inadvertently complete an agreement to provide design services and then, to their dismay, discover that no principal or employee within the firm has sufficient knowledge or experience to properly formulate the design. A frantic search for sufficiently qualified personnel is conducted in an effort to extricate themselves from a situation they could have easily anticipated. The lack of experienced professionals causes the temptation to arise to try to muddle through somehow, produce the best design possible under the circumstances, and hope for the best.

The professional liability risks you create by this course of action defy calculation. An unlimited confidence in the abilities of your staff, unsupported by fact, constitutes a poor basis for a decision to accept work. Following this path may well result in the floundering, and possible disappearance, of a design professional practice which is furnishing a sorely needed service.

Perhaps it is improbable this series of events would occur in your office. The example, however, serves to illustrate a common weakness among design professionals: the inability to recognize the limits of their firm's capabilities. Principals often lose sight of whether or not back-up personnel are available in the event of the departure of a well-qualified person with unique experience. If you consider your operation a team effort, evaluate the quality and number of substitutes available in the event of a casualty to one of your key players.

Re-examine your personnel qualification records and review the academic and experience history of each of your project designers before accepting new projects. Never commit yourself to an obligation you are unable to fulfill. You may have the personnel, but they may already be fully committed.

One area of concern which influences the risk of legal involvement is the misrepresentation of your professional capabilities. A few design professional firms overstate their qualifications in telephone directories, engineering directories or in brochures and proposals that they present to interested potential clients. They often misstate their firm's capabilities by sheer inadvertence. Some unique qualifications may be contained in a brochure which is several years old and the personnel possessing those qualities are no longer with the firm. In order that you not misrepresent your capabilities in this way, it is critical to keep your firm's list of qualifications up to date. Some firms avoid the permanently bound type of brochure; instead they select binding methods that permit the removal of obsolete data and the insertion of new data, accurately setting out their capabilities and experience.

Sell but do not oversell

Remember, if you are sued, your performance will be judged by the use of the legal standard of care, that is, the care exercised by the average professional offering the same services in the community. If you have any doubt at all about your ability to perform in a complete and competent fashion the services you offer, you would be far better off refusing the job. The risk is not worth the possible gain.

The risk is not worth the gain

Assemble your personnel qualification records and re-examine your company brochure with an eye toward eliminating inaccurate statements about your firm's ability. Then ask yourself, "If a lawsuit occurred involving claims of professional negligence, have I made any statement in the brochure which would mislead anyone about my present capabilities?" A judge and jury will give little sympathy to the excuse that, "I did have personnel qualified to handle that type of project when the brochure was first published, but they are no longer with the firm. When the client offered me this project, I thought I could hire qualified personnel to do this type of design." A brochure is a statement of your present qualifications and your past experience. Evaluate your representations to the public by objective standards and avoid costly and time-consuming misunderstandings.

D. Bidding

A prospective client unfamiliar with your firm asks you to state your fee for performing certain design services but expresses no interest whatever in your qualifications. Does such an approach arouse suspicion in your mind? If your answer is "Yes," you are speaking loss prevention language. That type of inquiry is a clue that the project may be underfinanced and therefore undesirable from a claims viewpoint, as indicated earlier.

Unfortunately there are some clients who have sufficient funds to construct a good quality project but who are not aware that the expenditures to obtain design excellence can actually result in lower first cost to the owner even after adding the cost of the design services. These misled clients require information and explanation which only you can give. Some can become loyal and profitable clients if they realize that their misplaced emphasis on low cost design is, in the final analysis, costing them dollars. Other prospective clients refuse to realize the disservice to themselves effected by this obsession with low cost design services. They consistently seek fee quotations which are quite properly termed bids. A business arrangement conducted in this manner may not be illegal, but it does dilute efforts to preserve quality as the basis for choosing a design professional.

Design professionals in the past have pointed to the undesirable characteristics of bidding for design services, frequently mentioning that such conduct is a breach of ethics that results in the client's receiving less than he should for his money. Equally important (or perhaps more important) and often overlooked, are the professional liability aspects of this style of business practice.

The connection between bidding for design services and professional liability claims is best illustrated by observing a typical bidding transaction. One common

Higher first cost may result in total lower costs

variety begins with a prospective client who wishes to retain your firm to perform design services. During the discussion, the prospective client carefully emphasizes such considerations as the prestige of the project, the public relations value of having one's name associated with such a project, and the likelihood of additional work of a much more profitable nature. The prospective client then may tell you that you are not the first firm to have been contacted, and that he has been dissatisfied with the past services performed for him by one of your competitors. Finally when the magic word "fee" is mentioned, the prospective client tells you he would be willing to consider retaining you provided your fee is "reasonable." He then points out the relative simplicity of the design tentatively proposed for the particular project, inferring that little effort would be needed to perform the services. Up to this moment, many of the characteristics of a standard negotiation are present. At this point, however, the prospective client might say, "One of your competitors who did our work previously charged us X percent of the actual construction cost for their work even though the projects were not complicated. If you will agree to do it for one-half percent less, the project is yours and remember, if you do a good job, there may be more work where this came from."

Most design professionals would be offended by such a statement and would break off negotiations at this stage. If asked for the reason, the design professional would reply that he could not do a good job at such a low fee and that it would be unethical to accept work on that basis. He often fails to consider, much less mention, that such projects are usually of the claims-producing variety.

As noted earlier, an owner or client who chooses to cut corners in this way may be operating with insufficient funds to produce a good quality project. This consuming concern with cost reduction induces the application of the same tactics for the retention of design services as for contracting. As soon as you discover you are expected to work for a fee lower than you feel is minimum, and are nevertheless tempted to accept the offer, stop for a moment and

We will make you famous

He who asks you to bid, asks you to gamble

85

weigh the expected benefits against your liability exposure. Your professional future could easily rest on this decision.

A client who requests that you submit a bid suffers from the same lack of knowledge of your professional function as the client who offers you an inadequate fee. In both cases, the client mistakenly believes he can cut down in overall cost by minimizing your fee. You should handle both types of clients in the same way. For example, one design professional responds to a request for a bid figure in the following manner:

> Your letter describing the project you plan to build arrived yesterday. Thank you for considering our firm to do the design planning. It sounds like the type of project we would enjoy. A look at our schedule shows that we could begin preliminary studies soon.
>
> One problem, however, gives some difficulty. You have asked that we submit a bid for our services and we are unable to do this. Even though we feel that we are well-qualified to do this type of job, we would be working against your interests by competing with other firms for your project on the basis of the lowest fee. Why? Because the total cost of the project (including our fees) may actually be **reduced** by more thorough design planning. When a reduction in the design fee is made in an effort to cut total costs, it may actually defeat that purpose.
>
> Your principal aim, we know, is to obtain both a trouble-free project and one that is constructed at economical cost. You need someone with the design capabilities to make this result more likely. The brochure we are enclosing outlines our qualifications. After you read it, we hope you will select our firm to do the job. If so, we would be happy to negotiate a fee for our services with you. Not all of the information you might need to make your decision is contained in the brochure, so we plan to call you before the end of the week with information about recent, satisfied clients that you might find interesting.

Answers to the request for a bid

A bid from an engineer creates an incentive to cut corners

We look forward to further discussions with you and hope we can be of service.

As you can see, this is an effort to educate rather than to scold or criticize. It is a professional approach. It is also the professional liability-conscious approach.

E. Adoption — Limitation of Liability

The seeds of professional liability problems may be sown in the development of the client long before a project is actually underway. The fruit borne of misunderstandings in the initial stages of the relationship may be bitter indeed some years later.

No design professional avows that he is perfect, nor should the law expect him to be. Nevertheless, by his attitude, as well as what he says, the design professional often produces the impression that no one should — or would — question his work.

Misunderstanding — the root of the problem

It is expected that the professional will exercise his best judgment and care in preparing designs and selecting materials, and that he will perform in accordance with generally accepted standards within his community. But by the very nature of the business, construction practices, techniques, and materials are constantly undergoing change, improvement, and modification. It is the design professional's job not just to follow the old tried and true formulas, but to use creative judgment and thought in developing innovations and applying new ideas. Originally, professional liability insurance was designed to provide for those few occasions when an honest error was made, or when, despite the most careful research and study, a new idea did not work out as well as expected.

Progress — a characteristic of the design profession

In recent years the situation has changed considerably. There is a growing tendency to sue for damages whenever the unexpected occurs, or because of dissatisfaction. The result has been that design professionals are being sued with increasing frequency — not only for legitimate reasons, but because of the legal ploy of suing anyone connected with a project in hopes that someone will be made to pay. This trend has received impetus from judgments rendered by lay juries and judges who have been bewildered by the technical facts and have felt sympathy for someone claiming injury. Thus, the design professional in private practice today finds himself faced with the possibility of having to answer extravagant, and often unfounded, claims for errors, omissions or professional negligence. Frequently these claims result from construction or materials failures over which he has little or no control. However, he **did** have control over the relationship and understanding with the client **PRIOR** to the problem arising.

1. Problem

Doctrine of fault

Our present legal system is not responsive to professional liability problems. Much of the trouble seems to lie in the fact that our unintentional tort law is based upon a fault doctrine. This holds, in effect, that a wronged party may seek redress from another who has negligently breached a duty (i.e. been at fault), thereby causing him damages. It is the failure of this concept that causes much of the problem. Fault is a subjective quality, and so the law has a way of creating a fiction in an effort to find fault in situations when the duty and fault relationship is inappropriate. This is hurting the design professional.

Some U. S. judges and juries believe fault must exist if someone suffers a loss. Plaintiff's attorneys take advantage of this in developing their bargaining power. They reason, "The larger the claim, the greater our bargaining power." As a consequence, when a party is involved in litigation, it is common practice for the plaintiff's attorney to inflate the damages as much as possible to create a bargaining advantage. Unfortunately, the complexities of modern day litigation are such that judge and jury alike may confuse these inflated claims for damages as somehow related to the extent of "fault" on the part of the defendant. It is in this strange network of tangled legal doctrines that the design professional practices his profession — a profession connected with activity in which the unexpected frequently occurs.

2. Possible Remedies

It is not likely that design professionals are going to be able to exert sufficient pressure on the mentors of our legal system to change the situation. Consequently, they must use other devices in order to create a more favorable environment for their practice. Limitation of liability is one such device; a technique which is now recognized and used by such claims-susceptible businesses and industries as maritime shipowners, SEC lawyers, financial analysts, international airlines, interstate truckers, parking-lot operators, and hotels. This concept implies a belief that a person acting in good faith on behalf of another will be responsible in reasonable measure to that second person, but should not be jeopardized by enormous penalties when unexpected contingencies occur. Limitation of liability, as espoused by design professionals, would establish a reasonable assumption of liability on their part in proportion to their fee. It would have the effect of bringing some types of claims for damages back into a reasonable perspective so that the issues involved could be faced on a more realistic and less expensive basis, and still be equitable to all parties concerned.

Limitation of liability is time-tested

Present professional liability trends are becoming increasingly detrimental to the design professional. Something must be done, and soon, if he is to maintain his place in our society. Limitation of liability gives him a ready answer; all he need do is use it, and the best and easiest time to use it is in the client development stage. From the beginning the design professional must make sure that the client understands his duties and responsibilities as well as the limits thereof. If he has "set the stage" well, the acceptance of the limitation of liability concept should be easy. The following pages are designed as suggestions for implementation of limitation of liability. It is hoped that the ideas contained in the text will explain the positive and beneficial effects it may bring to all parties connected with the construction process.

3. Limitation of Liability

    Your clients are not all alike. Each has his own special considerations, his own point of view, and his own past experience. His acceptance of limitation of liability is easier or harder, depending on his background.

    In spite of the diversity of the clients with whom you work, the reasons why they should adopt limitation of liability may be common to all, but may simply need to be expressed in different terms. Let us first look at the negative side:

Questions you may face

    *   Changing the status quo on anything is difficult. There must be good and convincing reasons for making changes.

    *   People are suspicious of new contract language. They are inclined to ask themselves, "What's in it for me?" and at the same time think, "What's in it for him?"

    *   If they think they are giving something up, they will think, "Why should I do this?"

    Any communications aimed at implementing limitation of liability should anticipate the foregoing questions. It is the same as convincing any person, used to old procedures, that a new way to handle an old problem might be the best.

    Limitation of liability in your contract of hire is fair. Usually a client will accept it as a condition precedent to your performing work if it is properly explained to him. The attributes of limitation of liability work in his favor. If these advantages, plus your reasons for adopting them are delineated, your client should be willing to accept the limitation as a normal way of doing business.

How to

    Let us examine some of the methods being employed by design professionals who have gained acceptance of limitation of liability in their contracts of hire.

a. Small Client — Single Project

Frequently on a small project it is difficult to enter into a lengthy, written contract. Yet there are important considerations of which both parties should be aware. In this situation, it is recommended that the design professional use a letter proposal and agreement form or work agreement form which spells out the most important factors connected with the work. These documents should include a limitation of liability clause along with a short explanation that your professional association has adopted such clauses as standard operating procedure. Some use a letter proposal similar to Exhibit 7. A sample work agreement is shown as Exhibit 8.

EXHIBIT 7

SMALL CLIENT PROPOSAL LETTER AND AGREEMENT FORM

Subject: Proposal For Services

Gentlemen:

Project:

We are pleased to submit this proposal for services to be performed for (description of project: name, type, location, etc.)

Scope of Services:

We will perform services necessary to accomplish the purposes set forth above. The scope of our services will include: (Give a clear description of the scope of services.)

Fees:

A. If you use a schedule of charges, the following paragraph might be appropriate.

We propose that our fees be computed on a time and expense basis in accordance with our schedule of charges (copy enclosed). Based on estimated (time and personnel would be included at this point), we estimate our charges to be in the order of $ _____ .

B.   *If you do not use a schedule or charges, the following paragraph may be useful.*

Fees for all services outlined above will be charged on an hourly basis at the rate of 2.53 x direct personnel expense of staff members working on your project (or your current fee schedule). Once the scope of work is defined, maximum estimated fees for services can be established. It is difficult to estimate a maximum fee without a thorough knowledge of your requirements. However, for planning purposes, (at this point give the client some idea of what you think the fees will be). We will invoice you monthly for the work and expenses incurred during the preceding month.

Payment is due (as per your usual practice).

Terms and Conditions:

A.   *If you use standard conditions, you may wish to append and incorporate these by reference. For example:*

To assure a clear understanding of all matters related to our mutual responsibilities, the appended Standard Conditions For Design Professionals' Services are made a part of this agreement for our services.

B.   *If you do not use standard conditions, the conditions should be spelled out in the letter.*

C.   *In either event, the terms and conditions should include the following paragraphs.*

Limitation of Liability: The Owner agrees to limit the Design Professional's liability to the Owner and to all construction Contractors and Subcontractors on the project, due to the Design Professional's negligent acts, errors or omissions, such that the total aggregate liability of each Design Professional to all those named shall not exceed $50,000 or _____, whichever is greater.

In the blank use one of the following phrases:

- the Design Professional's total fee for services rendered on this project;

- a percentage of the cost of construction for that part of the project designed by the Professional.

  If this proposal meets your approval, please sign where noted below, and return a copy to our office to serve as our authorization.

Thank you for considering us for this work. We look forward to working with you.

Respectfully submitted,

(your name)

AUTHORIZATION

Signature for (client stamp or name)

Date

EXHIBIT 8

SMALL CLIENT CONTRACT AGREEMENT FORM

CONTRACT AGREEMENT TO ENGAGE THE SERVICES OF _____ AS A CONSULTANT AND ADVISOR.

This agreement, entered into at _____

on the _____ day of _____, 19 _____,

between _____ hereinafter

called "Client," and _____

hereinafter called "Design Professional," is as follows:

The Client and Design Professional, for mutual consideration hereinafter set forth, agree as follows:

A. The Design Professional agrees to perform certain consulting, design, advisory, and/or surveying services for the Client as follows: *(Give a clear and detailed description of the scope of services to be rendered at this point.)*

B. Client agrees to pay the Design Professional as compensation for his services as follows: *(Set out in some detail the timing and method of charging and the method by which you wish to be paid. Also include finance charges in monthly percentage rates and the percentage rate per year. You may wish to include language concerning litigation and collection expenses.)*

C. Conditions: *If you wish to incorporate standard provisions used by your firm, use the following sentence:*

The standard provisions (attached, or set forth upon the reverse side hereof) are here incorporated into and made a part of this agreement.

If you do not use standard provisions, then the provisions and conditions must be set out individually.

In either case, include the following paragraph as a condition:

The Owner agrees to limit the Design Professional's liability to the Owner and to all construction Contractors and Subcontractors on the project, due to the Design Professional's negligent acts, errors or omissions, such that the total aggregate liability of each Design Professional to all those named shall not exceed $50,000 or _____, whichever is greater.

In the blank above, select one of the phrases below:

• the Design Professional's total fee for services rendered on this project; or

• a percentage of the cost of construction for that part of the project designed by the professional.

_____   _____
Signature of Firm   Date

_____
Signature of Client

b. Large Client — Large Project

While it may seem to you that large clients would be less inclined to limit your liability, experience to date proves this not to be so. The more sophisticated the buyers of design professonals' services are, the more they understand the need for limitation of liability in the contract of hire. Frequently, larger clients will forward any documents dealing with contractual matters to an attorney for his approval. Keep in mind that any communication you send to your client will be reviewed by his attorney. This makes it incumbent on you to point out to your large client the positive features of limitation of liability so that they will be clearly evident to the attorney when he is making his judgment on the advisability of limitation of liability. Your letter of transmittal should contain information which demonstrates to the large client (and his attorney) that:

Sophisticated clients are more likely to understand limitation of liability

- Limitation of liability is reasonable in amount: $50,000 or your fee. (Your fee may be substantially greater than $50,000 and well within the realm of what would be considered "reasonable" in light of the work to be performed.)

- By limiting liability, the large client maintains a lower level of fee structure than might otherwise be possible.

- Point out that limiting liability, and passing the same limitation on to the contractor or subcontractor who performs the work, contributes to the quality of the work performed and peace of mind of the client. This is so, since most contracts are let to bid. Incompetent or unscrupulous contractors may bid low and then seek extras by claiming that your client's plans and specifications (prepared by you) contained errors and omissions which caused him to underbid the work; that because of this, he will require extras (effectively raising his bid price to a more profitable level). By having limitation of liability in the general conditions, this practice is obviated, or at least mitigated, to an amount that will be easier to cope with if litigation should ensue.

This should have powerful appeal not only to your client, but to any attorney who is desirous of representing his client's best interests. A sample contract transmittal form is shown in Exhibit 9.

EXHIBIT 9

LARGE CLIENT CONTRACT TRANSMITTAL FORM

Subject: Contract for Professional Services

Dear (Large Client):

We have returned the contract which you sent us for execution. In accordance with your instructions, we have made the additions we feel necessary in the form of an addendum and duplicated our execution on that page. One of these, the limitation of liability clause, has now become standard in the contracts used by the members of (name of the appropriate organization endorsing this). As we mentioned to you, if this clause is unacceptable, it will be necessary for us to increase our fee slightly.

There are several reasons why you should look affirmatively on this clause. Not the least of these is that the project you are about to undertake will be *let to open competitive bid*. This means that a wide range of contractors may seek to perform the work. Some will be better qualified than others. In the past, similar projects have been extremely harsh on the design team and posed unexpected financial burdens on their clients. The reason? In their zeal to secure the work, certain contractors have bid too low a figure. Thereafter, finding themselves in financial difficulty, they alleged that the plans and specifications supplied to them by the owner were insufficient, contained errors or omissions, or were in some other manner defective. We believe that it would be prudent for you to put a curb on these practices. It is our proposal that this be accomplished by your acceptance of our clause and that a similar clause be included in the general conditions for the contractor and subcontractors to execute.

We believe that you recognize that we are not attempting to shirk any responsibility. It should be the contractor's duty to prepare his bid in a precise manner. If discrepancies are noted by him, he should seek clarification (as already required by the general conditions), to preclude the chance of later financial surprises that could be inimical to your interests. The limitation we are seeking is reasonable. It allows you to maintain a lower fee structure for our services. It will help eliminate requests of dubious value for extras by contractors because of alleged defects in the plans and specifications. We recommend that you include it in our contract.

(Cover other items about the contract and the work to be performed.)

Yours truly,

c. Continuing Clients

Frequently you work for clients on a continuing basis. Once the terms and conditions of your employment are understood, you do not enter into specific agreements on new jobs. It is good practice, however, to refresh the details of your employment in writing at least once a year. It is at this point that you should explain limitation of liability in its simplest terms and include it in your renewal agreement as a condition which will be present in all future work. A sample is shown in Exhibit 10.

Annual review

EXHIBIT 10

CONTINUING CLIENTS
RENEWAL AGREEMENT

Dear _____:

We have worked with you for _____ years and have greatly appreciated the business you have given us. We have also greatly enjoyed the fine working relationship we have had with you. This has evolved in the absence of written contracts, and we would like to keep it that way.

As you know, all professionals have a problem: professional liability claims. These have increased astronomically in the last 20 years. This has been the experience of the majority of professions: doctors, lawyers, accountants and design professionals. While our firm has had very little trouble in this respect, others have experienced quite a bit. It has become apparent that many claims have been entered for the sole purpose of establishing a plaintiff's bargaining position, and not because of merit. Because of this, the experience has been that the vast majority of claims have been successfully defended. But the costs of such defense have been extraordinarily high. In light of this, many professional organizations are promoting the limitation of liability concept.

We strongly feel that the adopton of limitation of liability would be mutually beneficial to both of us, and, more widely, the whole construction industry. In light of this feeling, we would like to adopt it as part of our understanding with you.

Will you please let us know your feelings on this matter. Your early attention to this would be greatly appreciated.

Very truly yours,

---

d. Governmental Agencies

If much of your work is done for governmental agencies, you may believe that limitation of liability is not applicable to your practice. Nothing could be further from the truth. Governmental bodies, more than any other client, are possible beneficiaries of the effectiveness of limitation of liability. After all, you are **their agent.** Any claim made against you affects them. They are all subjected to a sequence of factors similar to the following: as a governmental body they **must** let all of their work be the subject of competitive bids. When the bids are received, if the bidding contractor has the necessary bonding, they **must** award the contract to the low bidder. Low bidders on governmental work frequently seek to recoup any losses they may suffer on a job by alleging that the plans and specifications were not fit and sufficient for the purpose intended. If you doubt the authenticity of the foregoing scenario, ask the contract administrator of a governmental agency for whom you do design work. His experience probably will be replete with examples of being subjected to claims by contractors who have underbid jobs and then sought to recover on the basis that the government office provided them with plans and specifications that were not fit and sufficient for the purpose intended. By explaining the simplicity of limitation of liability and how it will work to negate this practice, you should receive their blessing. This will be even more true if you are able to demonstrate that your professional society has adopted it as a standard practice.

The letter as shown in Exhibit 11 is representative of the type that might be written in connection with the transmittal of a contract of hire with a governmental agency. This Exhibit is framed for a California design professional, and would require modification in other states.

Great advantage to governmental clients

EXHIBIT 11

GOVERNMENTAL AGENCY LETTER FORM

Subject: Contract for Professional Services

Dear _____:

We have gone over the contract of hire which you sent for the work connected with *(name of project)*. We find it to be substantially in compliance with our intent, and our insurance broker advises us that the hold harmless and indemnity provision is not in contravention with our insurance. We would like to ask two things: 1) Since we will have substantial work product invested in the job prior to its completion, we would like to be named on the Builders Risk "All Risk" policy during course of construction as an insured. This will serve to protect our interest should an untimely catastrophe befall the project prior to its acceptance, and 2) Our professional association, *(name of appropriate organization)*, has recommended that its members use a limitation of liability clause in their contracts of hire. We have appended a copy of this clause for your consideration. If the *(name of governmental agency)* is willing to include this clause in our contract of hire and put it in the General Conditons to be used on the project, we will be willing to reduce our quoted fee by _____ %.

There are several reasons why you should look affirmatively on this clause. First, California Law specifically provides for such a clause (Cal. Civ. Code Section 2782.5). Second, as mentioned above, its adoption allows a lower fee structure for our services. Third, the project you are about to undertake must be let to open competitive bid. A wide variety of contractors may seek to perform this work. Some will be better qualified than others. However, in light of the Supreme Court's Opinion in *City of Inglewood — Los Angeles County Civic Center Authority, et. al. v. The Superior Court of Los Angeles County,* _____ Cal 3d _____ (1972), you are required to accept the lowest bid. As you know, in their zeal to secure the work, certain contractors bid too low. Thereafter, finding themselves in financial difficulties, they sue for extras alleging that the plans and specifications supplied to them by the government contained errors or omissions, or were in some other manner defective. This practice is extremely harsh on all parties, imposing unexpected financial burdens on the design team and the government, and sowing acrimony among all parties. We believe that your acceptance of our clause and inclusion of a similar clause in the General Conditions for the contractor and subcontractor will put a curb on such a practice.

Please recognize that we are not attempting to shirk any responsibility. It is the contractor's duty to prepare his bid accurately. If discrepancies are noted by him in the plans and specifications, he should seek clarification (as already required by the General Conditions). This would preclude the chance of later financial surprises which would be inimical to your interests. The limitation we seek is reasonable. It is provided for by law. It allows us to maintain a lower fee structure for our services. It will help eliminate requests of dubious value for extras by contractors because of alleged defects in the plans and specifications.

(Cover other items about the contract and the work to be performed.)

Very truly yours,

e. Another Design Professional As A Client

If another design professional is your client, will the limitation of liability concept still work? Certainly, but one additional step is necessary. The client must include the limitation of liability provision in his agreement with the owner. By so doing, the client will also benefit from the protection it offers.

Once your client understands the limitation of liability concept, you can expect assistance rather than resistance. Experienced design professionals should be anxious to join you in your efforts to bring reason back into the profession of designing structures. Most are painfully aware of the spectre of legal involvement, and are seaching diligently for fair and reasonable limits to their liability.

Once understood, the limitation of liability concept sells itself

Invite your clients to review the written material on the subject and to view available audio-visual programs which explain the fundamentals of the limitation of liability concept. Plan group meetings and make limitation of liability one of the prime topics of discussion.

The design professional who is your client should also explain limitation of liability to his owner-clients. By helping him convince the owners of the benefits of limitation of liability, both of you will be helped.

Your clients will be interested to know that design professional organizations have adopted limitation of liability as recommended standard practice for their members. Limitation of liability is not new. Some design professionals have been using standard limitation of liability provisions in their design services agreement forms for several years without experiencing difficulty with clients.

Mutual assistance among design professionals has always been worthwhile. Making limitation of liability a standard provision in all agreements for design services is another means of encouraging harmony and strengthening ties between the design professions. A sample letter to a design professional client is shown in Exhibit 12.

EXHIBIT 12

LIMITATION OF LIABILITY LETTER TO A DESIGN PROFESSIONAL CLIENT

Dear _____:

As you know, everyone in the design professions is concerned about the problem of professional liability claims. Not only do we find that we have to pay greater sums for our professional liability insurance, but we are now faced with reductions in coverage, and the constant spectre of being involved in lengthy, fruitless litigation.

Recently, a group of professional associations and at least one professional liability insurance underwriter have made a suggestion which they hope will have a major impact on this situation. They are relying upon a technique which has a lengthy history and wide acceptance in other professions and businesses: limitation of liability.

It is the assessment of the organizations that have studied our problem that many of the claims brought against us are either poorly founded, or exaggerated in scope. By limiting our liability to a stated amount, it is the feeling that both the frequency and the severity of our claims will be reduced.

Our firm would like to make use of limitation of liability as a professional liability loss prevention tool. In order to do so, since you are our client and the prime design professional, it must be a concept to which you will agree.

If limitation of liability appeals to you, please let me know, and we will supply you with further details concerning its use in practice.

Yours truly,

f.   The Contractor

The foregoing pages may sound as though a heavy burden is being placed upon the man who does the work — the contractor. This is not so. Limitation of liability does not make him responsible for your errors, omissions, or negligence. If he performs the work in accordance with your plans and specifications and they contain errors and omissions, that is not his responsibility. He has done all that may be expected of him. It is probable that the only source of **damages** that he might suffer from errors or omissions in the plans and specifications would be if he bid too low on a job and later sought to recoup on account of alleged failures in the plans and specifications. A contractor who signs a contract which contains a limitation of liability clause running

The benefit accrues to reputable contractors

in favor of the owner and the design professional is agreeing to limit the amount of **damages** that he will be entitled to because of deficiencies in the designs and specifications. He in no way is assuming liability for damages to other parties.

What has been said of previous parties might be said about the contractor. Limitation of liability is not adverse to his interests. It has positive features that should make it attractive to him as a businessman. Not the least of these has been pointed out by contractors who have accepted limitation of liability. They contend that they are tired of bidding for jobs which are taken away from them by lowballers (either bidding low intentionally or through lack of understanding) who thereafter, during the course of construction, seek extras that would, in effect, have made their bid higher had they prepared a credible figure. Limitation of liability will stem the practice of bidding low and seeking to recoup losses at a later date. This will benefit the honest and competent contractor who has the necessary skill to prepare a bid that is well-conceived and accurate in its sum. Explain to contractors who work on your designs that limitation of liability does not make them liable for your errors, omissions and deficiencies in design, nor does it require special insurance. It merely places them in the position of doing that which they should be doing anyway, bidding accurately and honestly. This should make them willing to accept it. They will recognize that it will aid them in their attempt to weed out unscrupulous bidders.

The general conditions phraseology shown in Exhibit 13 may be of assistance.

EXHIBIT 13

LIMITATION OF LIABILITY
IN CONTRACTOR'S
GENERAL CONDITIONS

Version 1.

The Contractor (and his Subcontractors) is (are) skilled and experienced in the use and interpretation of plans and specifications such as those included in the bid documents for this contract. He has (They have) carefully reviewed the plans and specifications and has (have) found them free of ambiguities and sufficient for bid purposes. Further, he has (they have) based his (their) bid solely on those documents not relying in any way on any explanation or interpretation, oral or written, from any other source. Having assured himself of the adequacy of the documents and the accuracy of his bid, the Contractor agrees (and shall require his Subcontractors to agree) to limit the liability of the Design Professional and the Owner for negligence, errors or omissions of the Design Professional to a total aggregate sum of $50,000 or _____ whichever is greater. The Contractor (and his Subcontractors) does (do) not assume any liability for damages to others caused by the negligence, errors or omissions of the Design Professional.

Version 2.

(Includes bidder observation of site and materials.) The Bidder is skilled and experienced in the use and interpretation of plans and specifications. He has carefully reviewed the plans and specifications for this project and has found them to be free of ambiguities and sufficient for bid purposes. Further, he has carefully examined the site of the work and, from his own observations, has satisfied himself as to the nature and location of the work; the character, quality and quantity of materials; the difficulties likely to be encountered; and other items which may affect the performance of the work. He has based his bid solely on these documents and observations and has not relied in any way on any explanation or interpretation, oral or written, from any other source. Therefore, the Bidder agrees to limit the liability of the Design Professional and the owner for negligence, errors or omissions of the Design Professional to a total aggregate sum of $50,000 or _____ whichever is greater. The Bidder in no way assumes liability for damages to others for the negligence, errors, or omissions of the Design Professional.

Version 3. (Short Form)

The Contractor is experienced in the use and interpretation of plans and specifications such as those included in the Project Bid Documents. He has carefully reviewed the project plans and specifications and has found them to be free of ambiguity and sufficient for bid purposes. He has based his bid solely on these documents, not relying on any explanation or interpretation from any other source. The Contractor, therefore, agrees to limit liability of the Design Professional and the owner for damages to him because of the negligence, errors or omissions of that Design Professional to an aggregate total of $50,000 or _____ , whichever is greater. In doing so, the Contractor does not assume any liability for damages to others caused by the negligence, errors, or omissions of the Design Professional.

In the blank above, select one of the phrases below;

- Design Professional's total fee for services rendered on this project; or

- Percent of the total cost of construction for that part of the project designed by the Design Professional.

g. Groups

It is an interesting phenomenon that it is sometimes easier to communicate with people in groups than on an individual basis. Why this is so is a mystery. Human beings tend to be more receptive in groups when offered a suggestion than as individuals. This is one reason why limitation of liability should be discussed with clients, governmental bodies, contractors, and members of the public through their associations, public hearings, or specially convened meetings. In such instances, it is good practice to use all available material.

There are several forms of material that might be used in group discussions of limitation of liability. These include 35mm slides and a script written with various audiences in mind (owners, contractors, and members of the public). In addition, pamphlets on limitation of liability are available. Not to be overlooked are design professionals who are knowledgeable in limitation of liability. Many have a particular knack for explaining the intricacies involved. Some have volunteered to make time available (with sufficient notice) to speak before groups who may be interested in limitation of liability. The value of these various means of disseminating information will be lost unless they are used. Please take advantage of all of them. The winner, if you do, will be **you.**

Communication aids

F. A Meeting of Minds? — Your Agreement

A written agreement is sometimes said to be useful only when there is a disagreement. Parenthetically we can add that as long as mutual understanding and an atmosphere of cooperation exist between you and your client, an oral agreement may be quite sufficient. Unfortunately, the smooth-running project is elusive these days. Due to rigid financial commitments and a general decline in the quality of workmanship and materials, it is increasingly rare for a professional to design a project of any reasonable magnitude without controversy resulting during the design period and the construction period.

These are trying times

The arrival of a summons and complaint usually means that the time for peaceful discussion of the problem is over. Your attorney will tell you that any litigation requires proof of your position. The job is made infinitely easier if your part of the bargain is set out in well-defined terms which do not rely upon the fading and convenient memories of the parties involved.

Fundamental though these statements may appear, the fact remains that substantial numbers of design professionals frequently render services on projects involving huge sums of money on the basis of a hand-shake. In no other area of the construction industry do the participants to an agreement involving large sums of money deal on such an informal basis. Your more business-oriented colleagues on the construction team, such as contractors and material suppliers, consider a well-drafted contract document **in writing** a necessity, not merely a convenience. Some design professionals, more worried about the possible adverse reaction of the client than about their own professional welfare, actually regard a requirement for a complete, well-written agreement as quite **in**convenient!

A written agreement
formalizes the informal

The list of arguments presented to persuade individuals to put their agreements in writing seldom includes one invaluable fringe benefit. When any agreement is reduced to writing, it is required that more detailed thought be given to the scope of the obligations and duties of the parties. As a consequence, one party may discover that his understanding of the limits of the agreement is quite different than what is understood by others. The writing procedure naturally leads to further negotiations until a satisfactory description of the terms and conditions are arrived at by the parties. The whole process can be described as expressing the informal in a formal manner, or more briefly, "formalizing the informal."

As guesswork has no place in an area so technical as designing, uncertainty has no place in agreeing what services are to be provided. Without a written agreement, the determination of the scope of services may be left in the hands of a jury, and you may discover that they think you agreed to much more than you **ever** intended.

However, a one-sided contract can be worse than no contract at all. The one-sided contract, or unconscionable contract as it is sometimes called, results in the removal of "mutuality" from the transaction. You may be placed under a much heavier burden of performance than you should be.

If, in reading a proffered document, you discover that your own duties and obligations are quite extensive and set out in great detail, but those of the client are quite limited, you should view such a document with considerable suspicion. Of course, whether a contract is distinctly one-sided depends on one's viewpoint. Your attorney, if experienced in contracts, should be particularly well-qualified to evaluate the fairness of a contract **if** you apprise him of all the facts.

At the initial stage, an overwhelming majority of written contracts offered by one party to another are too one-sided and require some modifications in order to be fair to both parties. In most other businesses, it is natural and expected for both parties to make changes, perhaps several times, before the agreement is satisfactory. Many design professionals, untutored in the subtleties of business, often treat a contract document presented to them as complete, except for their signature, as a "take-it-or-leave-it" proposition. They are reluctant to negotiate and regard it as distasteful to haggle over details. If you are numbered among that group, the spectre of professional liability claims may soon force you to conquer this reluctance. The next time you are pressed to sign a contract document drafted by your client, take time to read it with care. Then list in one column your duties and obligations and, in another column, those of the client. Armed with this information, you should be able to make a preliminary evaluation of the fairness of the contract. Your attorney's advice at this point is extremely valuable; legal implications of a serious nature, and of which you are completely unaware, can be detected by his trained eye. Many experienced attorneys are also skilled negotiators. Those individuals, with your assistance, can suggest modifications which may protect your interests and at the same time prove palatable to your client.

Contracts have to be bilateral to be fair

This preventive legal treatment is easily worth the investment if it results in only a single instance where possible litigation is averted. Bear in mind that the more familiar your attorney is with your prospective contractual commitments, the more effective he can be.

109

G. The Scope of Your Services

Perhaps one of the areas of greatest concern from a professional liability point of view is the claim that is brought by an owner or contractor who has alleged that you have not lived up to your commitment. That is why it is extremely dangerous for you to take any type of work which reduces the scope of services which are normal and usual to the practice in your particular locality. Defense attorneys will advise that it is virtually impossible for you to escape the liability that is the result of failures in the construction review merely because you have not contracted to perform that service. This is generally true of all of the various services that design professionals offer.

This, then, means that the expansion of duties and responsibilities in today's changing world creates innumerable exposures to professional liability based upon allegations of failure to perform certain duties. With the energy crunch, environmental impact, project programming, landscape design, etc. all becoming part of a complete design professional's package, the chance that you will get sued for failure to perform one of these duties, even though you were not hired to do it, becomes very real.

There is an answer. It is a very good answer and it dovetails nicely with a better way of computing your fee. It is embodied in a technique which the California Council of the American Institute of Architects developed in 1973. They produced a document titled "Guidelines for Estimating Cost of Professional Services" that quite by chance created an excellent professional liability loss prevention tool for those claims where the allegation is failure in scope. They reason that a design professional should be paid greater or less depending upon the tasks he will perform. They devised a matrix which lists the services to be performed that enables the client to select which of these services the design professional will perform by checking an appropriate square. (Please see Exhibit 14.) If such a matrix is made part of your contract of hire, you have created an affirmative defense against those claims which arise from miscommunications about the scope of the intended services.

EXHIBIT 14

Document 100-73-A
©1973, CCAIA

COMPREHENSIVE ARCHITECTURAL SERVICES

FIRM:_____
CLIENT:_____
PROJECT:_____
LOCATION:_____

CONSULTANT SERVICES:

_____ Structural	_____ Mechanical	_____ Electrical	_____ Civil
_____ Acoustic	_____ Food Handling	_____ Traffic	_____ Landscape
_____ Hospital	_____ Educational	_____ Management	
_____ Other _____			

CLIENT RESPONSIBILITIES:

| _____ Site Survey | _____ Economic Feasibility | _____ Written Program |
| _____ Construction Manager | _____ Soils Investigation | _____ Budget |

COMPENSATION METHOD: Cost plus Professional Fee   Direct Personnel Expense   Other

Phase	Responsibility of			Date		SERVICES	Time Budget	Rate Charge	Compensation Based on:		Accrued Comp:
	Client	Arch't	Arch. to Coord.	Review w/Client	Activity Begins				Budgeted Time	Actual Time: Current Month	
I — PREDESIGN SERV.						1. Project Development Scheduling					
						2. Project Programming					
						3. Internal Function, Flow Studies/Space Plan.					
						4. Existing Building Surveys					
						5. Governmental Agency Consultation					
						6. Initial Concept and Budget Review					
						7. Economic Feasibility Analysis and Reports					
						8. Promo. Mats. Fund Raising/Project Financing					
						9. Administrative Services and Conferences					
						10. Principal's Time					
						11.					
						SUB TOTALS:					
II — SITE DEVELOPMENT						1. Site Analysis and Selection					
						2. Site Master Planning					
						3. Detailed Site Utilization Studies					
						4. On-Site Utility Studies					
						5. Off-Site Utility Studies					
						6. Zoning Analysis and Processing					
						7. Administrative Services and Conferences					
						8. Principal's Time					
						9.					
						SUB TOTALS:					
III — DESIGN SERVICES						1. Architectural Schematic Design					
						2. Engineering Systems Analyses					
						3. Architectural Design Development					
						4. Statement of Probable Construction Cost					
						5. Special Design					
						6. Landscape Design					
						7. Interior Design					
						8. Graphics Design					
						9. Furniture and Special Fixture Design					
						10. Renderings, Models and Mock-ups					
						11. Governmental and Regulatory Agency Review					
						12. Administrative Services and Conferences					
						13. Principal's Time					
						14.					
						SUB TOTALS:					
						GRAND TOTALS:					

COMPREHENSIVE ARCHITECTURAL SERVICES

Document 100-73-A
©1973, CCAIA

Phase	Responsibility of			Date		SERVICES	Time Budget	Rate Charge	Compensation Based on:		Accrued Comp:
	Client	Arch't	Arch. to Coord.	Reviewed w/Client	Activity Begins				Budgeted Time	Actual Time: Current Month	
IV – CONSTR. DOCUMENT						1. Architectural Working Drawings					
						2. Structural Working Drawings					
						3. Civil Working Drawings					
						4. Mechanical Working Drawings					
						5. Electrical Working Drawings					
						6. Specifications and General Conditions					
						7. Governmental/Regulatory Agency Approvals					
						8. Special Bid Documents					
						9. Final Statement of Probable Construction Cost					
						10. Administrative Services and Conferences					
						11. Principal's Time					
						12.					
						SUB TOTALS:					
V – BID. & NEG.						1. General Bidding Documents					
						2. General Construction Bidding					
						3. Negotiated Construction Bidding					
						4. Segregated Construction Bidding					
						5. Addenda and Drawing Revisions					
						6. Construction Agreement					
						7. Administrative Services and Conferences					
						8. Principal's Time					
						9.					
						SUB TOTALS:					
VI – CONSTRUCTION						1. Construction Contract Admin./Conferences					
						2. Construction Job Cost Accounting					
						3. Quotation Requests, Review/Change Orders					
						4. Clarifications					
						5. Shop Drawings and Submittal Review					
						6. Construction Observation and Certification					
						7. Testing and Inspection Coordination					
						8. Full Time Project Representation					
						9. Final Acceptance					
						10. Administrative Services and Conferences					
						11. Principal's Time					
						12.					
						SUB TOTALS:					
VII – POST CONST.						1. Maintenance and Operational Programming					
						2. As-Built Drawings					
						3. Warranty Reviews					
						4. Client Conferences					
						5. Administrative Services and Conferences					
						6. Principal's Time					
						7.					
						SUB TOTALS:					
VIII – SPEC. SERV.						1. Special Studies					
						2. Computer Applications					
						3. Fine Arts and Crafts					
						4. Expert Witness					
						5. Architectural Competition Advisor					
						6. Administrative Services and Conferences					
						7. Principal's Time					
						8.					
						SUB TOTALS:					
						GRAND TOTALS:					

A device was originated on the East Coast by at least one member of the ACEC that is similar in format. (Please see Exhibit 15. Note in particular the reference to limitation of liability; this form creates an excellent opportunity to introduce the subject.) We recommend that you follow a similar course of action in your practice with your clients. Make certain that the matrix or a similar form for designating responsibility is made a part of your contract of hire or is incorporated into it by reference. Documents such as these will give you a very good affirmative defense should someone allege that you are responsible for the performance of certain duties which have not been performed when in fact you were not hired to do them.

H. Contractual Pitfalls

Any type of threat arouses a defensive attitude in most of us. Frequently the response to threat is to overreact. Defensive overreactions have been widespread in the construction industry. Owners, plagued by runaway construction costs, poor results, and frequent claims have sought to defend themselves. Unfortunately, they have overreacted by adding restrictive covenants to all contracts of hire. These over-defensive clauses may be in the form of hold harmless agreements, warranties, or liquidated damage provisions, among others. While at one time these defensive covenants were limited to use between the owner and the contractor, increasingly they are finding their way into the contract between the owner and the design professional.

Restrictive contract provisions: harbingers of trouble

How should you, as a design professional, react when your client insists that you sign a contract containing one or more of these undesirable provisions? First, you should be certain that what is being asked of you is beyond the scope of your responsibility. Once defining what should and should not be your burden, you should take a polite but firm stand on any extension to your responsibility. This firm stand is mandatory especially in light of today's critical professional liability insurance situation. Frequently your insurance coverage is not broad enough to protect you against the liability you may assume in an unreasonable contract or agreement. Thus, it is in-

Do not assume responsibilities that are not yours

EXHIBIT 15

CARTER ENGINEERING, INC.
1107 Spring Street
SILVER SPRING, MD. 20910
301   588-3230

JOB

CLIENT:

ARCHITECT:

STRUCTURAL:

CIVIL:

LANDSCAPE:

SUBMITTED BY:

DATE:

ACCEPTED BY:

NAME:

TITLE:

DATE:

YES	NO	
_____	_____	Make Field Measurements — existing
_____	_____	Draw existing systems
_____	_____	Use of existing drawings
_____	_____	We Receive Utilities Site Plan
_____	_____	Red line on plans
_____	_____	Working Drawings
_____	_____	Paper By Others
_____	_____	Sepias By Others
_____	_____	We Provide Paper
_____	_____	Specification on drawings
_____	_____	Specification Master — CSI
_____	_____	Specification Master — Short Form
_____	_____	Shop drawing review
_____	_____	Const'n. Review, _____ Trips
_____	_____	Analysis of bids
_____	_____	Inspection & Report
_____	_____	Tenant Drawings
_____	_____	Cost Estimate
_____	_____	Plumbing, Inside
_____	_____	Plumbing, Site
_____	_____	Private Disposal System
_____	_____	Private Water System
_____	_____	Fire Protection System
_____	_____	Site Storm Drainage
_____	_____	Inside Storm Drainage
_____	_____	Soil Conservation
_____	_____	Htg., Vent'g., Air Cond'g.
_____	_____	Energy Conservation
_____	_____	Fuel Analysis
_____	_____	Electrical Power
_____	_____	Electrical Lighting
_____	_____	Site Lighting
_____	_____	Fire & Security System
_____	_____	Sound Systems
_____	_____	Telephone System
_____	_____	Power Study
_____	_____	Flat Fee
_____	_____	Percentage
_____	_____	D.P.E.
_____	_____	Partial Payments
_____	_____	Down Payment
_____	_____	Upset
_____	_____	1 ½ %/Month on Unpaid Balance
_____	_____	Payment at Time of Payment
_____	_____	Overtime Authorized
_____	_____	Limitation of Liability

Special Conditions:

cumbent upon you to remain on your guard at all times against these odious clauses. More specifically, watch out for the following:

- Hold Harmless and Indemnity Provisions
- Warranties and Guarantees
- Defense and indemnity Provisions
- Certification Clauses
- Certificates of Performance

How will you recognize such clauses? The following will serve as examples, but if there is any doubt in your mind, check with your attorney and insurance broker.

1. Hold Harmless and Indemnity Provisions

Words like "save harmless," "hold harmless," or "indemnify" sometimes show up in an agreement the design professional is asked to sign. Often, they are accompanied by other extreme words such as "any," "all," "whatsoever," "every," etc. None of these words belong in the prudent design professional's lexicon. When you see them in a contract and sign that contract, you may be agreeing to conditions that cannot be covered by your professional liability insurance.

There is one type of hold harmless agreement that your insurance may cover — where you agree to hold harmless and indemnify others from losses that arise from your own negligence or that of your employees. You would expect to be responsible for such losses, and the law requires you to be — with or without the clause. An insurable hold harmless and indemnification agreement might read as follows:

The Architect/Engineer hereby agrees to defend, indemnify, and save harmless, the Owner, its officers, agents, and employees, from and against any and all claims arising out of the negligent acts, errors, or omissions of the Architect/Engineer.

There are, however, at least four other types of hold harmless and indemnity provisions that you may face. These provisions have one thing in common. They all ask you to agree to the assumption of liabilities that would otherwise not be yours under the law. When you sign such agreements, you may be contracting away your legal rights and, with them, your insurance coverage. For example:

1. You agree to hold harmless and indemnify your client for liability arising out of your negligent acts, errors, or omissions or those of your client.

2. You agree to hold harmless and indemnify your client against any loss, injury, or damage arising out of your performance of the work.

3. You agree to hold harmless and indemnify your client against any losses resulting from acts, errors, or omissions of anyone performing work on the project. (Many states will not enforce this provision, or the one that follows, holding them to be against public policy.)

4. You agree to hold harmless and indemnify your client for all loss, injury, or damage arising out of the project, regardless of fault or cause. (Under such a clause, you assume strict liability for the entire project.)

An example of this last odious clause encountered in the fine print of a proposed agreement follows. Note particularly the extreme words.

> The Design Professional agrees to indemnify and save harmless the Owner from **any** and **all** liability, claims, demands, suits, actions, proceedings, loss, costs, and damage of **every** kind and description, including attorneys' fees, interest, court costs, and expense, which may be brought or made against the Owner because of injury or damage to persons (including claims

for the death of **any** person or persons) or property, received or sustained by reason of **any** acts or omissions of the Design Professional, contractor, subcontractor or subcontractors, or his or their employees, or the work itself, or **any** contingency arising therefrom.

Are you really insured?

Most underwriters are extremely cautious about what type of indemnity agreements they will insure. They do not want the design professional to shirk his burden of responsibility in any sense, but they are reluctant to insure liability which should not rightfully be his. Your thinking in regard to these clauses should mesh with their underwriting axioms.

2. Warranties and Guarantees

Some owners, after having been previously dissatisfied with their completed construction, have reacted by writing warranties and guarantees of performance into their subsequent contracts of hire. Usually these have been aimed at dissatisfaction with workmanship, but the development of the form has led to its inclusion in contracts with design professionals. Here again you must keep on your guard. The following exemplifies a warranty clause:

I promise

> The design professional warrants that all work performed on this project related to his design will conform to the drawings and specifications; futher, that it will be fit and sufficient for the purpose intended and operable in accordance with his design intent. The designer warrants that all services performed hereunder by himself, his employees or agents, will be performed by persons who are extraordinarily skilled in their profession and in accordance with the highest standards of workmanship in their field.

It's Superman!

Clauses such as the foregoing could spell serious professional liability insurance problems. The request that is made is tantamount to superhuman performance. It falls well outside of that which is reasonable in our business world. The design professional is hired for **his** skill. The level at which he performs is governed by matters implicit in law. Additions such as warranties and guarantees demean his professional status. Resist the inclusion of such clauses in your contract of hire.

3. Defense and Indemnity Provisions

The defense and indemnity provisions fall in the same family as hold harmless and indemnity agreements. They are typified by the following language:

> The design professional agrees to defend and indemnify the client against liability arising out of the performance of the work described herein.

Scrutinize these provisions and treat them as you would hold harmless and indemnity clauses. They may or may not be insurable. They hold a dubious place in a contract for professional services.

4. Certification Clauses and Certificates of Performance

A certificate is a written promise that some act has been or will be done. It is dissimilar to a written warranty in name only. It may come into a design professional's contract of hire by rote: that is, a corporation or governmental agency may, as a standard procedure, include a certification clause in all their contracts. Like the warranty clause, certification clauses and certificates of performance do not belong in a professional man's contract of hire since they frequently require a level of performance beyond that which should reasonably be expected.

It is unfortunate that with consultants, certain governmental agencies resist amending their contract of hire to eliminate these provisions. This seriously handicaps the design professional since it is doubtful that his professional liability underwriter will assume any liability imposed solely by the effect of a certification clause or provision. Certificates may take many forms. The following typifies one of these clauses:

You are put in the same bag

The design professional will certify, on the completion of the work, that all of the work has been performed in accordance with his plans and specifications and that any and all designs performed by this organization have been performed by persons most skilled in their discipline.

Remember, such certificates may expand your professional liability burden and therefore impede the effectiveness of your professional liability insurance coverage. Be alert to the presence of certificates in the contracts you sign. If you discover one, seek counsel from your attorney and your insurance broker so you may take steps to have it removed. If a client is aware that it reduces the effectiveness of insurance, he may remove it from your contract.

How do you handle a good client who wants you to hold him harmless, to give him a warranty, or to certify your work? Each contract will, by necessity, have to be treated differently. Personalities and the sensitivity of the client play an important part. Nonetheless, usually a client will be willing to listen and will accede to your wishes if you explain in logical terms why you should not be extending your liability. The following will give you a **successful** example of how this delicate subject has been handled by one firm:

The diplomatic approach

(This is an excerpt from their letter to a client.)

We recognize that this purchase order form has been specifically designed for the purchase of materials and equipment and that certain of the terminology are not normally contained in an Architecture/Engineer Agreement. We make particular reference to paragraph 6 which suggests a warranty that the services provided by us will be free of design defects. We are, of course, prepared to state that our design and specifications will be prepared in accordance with generally accepted professional architectural and engineering practices. A statement that they would be free of design defects is unrealistic. As in any field of expanding technology, each day brings knowledge of means of improving upon prior effort. Striving for improvement may result in incorporating new elements into a design which later proves to be less desirable than anticipated.

This same area of qualification may be touched on relative to paragraph 9 dealing with indemnification. We believe it quite proper that an indemnification clause be provided in areas in which we believe you are, in fact, immediately concerned. Those would be relative to negligent acts, errors, or omissions. In the broadest sense in which paragraph 9 could be interpreted, it would be, as an example, an indemnification against elements such as breach of contract or certain intentional torts. We do not believe that it is your intent to include such considerations.

That was one firm's approach that worked. Another design professional got the desired effect by the following:

We note that your contract of hire contains a hold harmless and indemnity clause. For several reasons we feel that this should be reversed. We are, after all, going to be lending you our expert help which requires that our highly qualified people be on your premises, where we have no control over the safety.

We will be subjected to operations in connection with the contractors you have hired and who are answerable only to you as respects the safety of the job site. Further, we will be exposed to suit by the contractor's workmen if they are injured, in their mistaken belief that we have some voice over the deportment of their employers.

For these reasons it seems proper for you to hold us harmless and indemnify us while we are performing services on your behalf. We recognize that such an idea might not be in keeping with your "standard form of agreement" so we will not insist upon this, but we must request that you, at least, delete the hold harmless and indemnity clause form from the contract which hires us to act in a professional capacity.

This letter made a lot of sense to the client. The argument succeeded because the design professional had an excellent rapport with his client. Although it might not be appropriate for general use, it does demonstrate an approach to clients in which the proper state of mind has been developed.

Good logic wins

I.   Estimating (Costs and Schedules)

When you present a proposed design to a client, invariably the first thing he wants to know is, "How much is it going to cost me?" The moment you give him a figure, you inherently create a potential claim situation. Why? Because most clients do not know the difference between a contractor's bid-quotation and a design professional's estimate.

When you make a cost estimate, you inherently create a potential claims situation

The difference should be carefully explained. The second question is often, "When will it be ready?" Each time you enter into an agreement to deliver the design portion of the construction contract documents on a certain date, you run the risk that you may be held responsible for a costly delay. Many claims against design professionals are based on the allegation of breach of contract, that is, failure to complete in the time agreed upon. Thus, estimating cost or time may be one of your most perilous professional acts.

Design professionals have the habit of being unduly optimistic in estimating. This is natural since there is reason to believe that optimism is an inherent quality of man. Social scientists speculate that optimism derives from an inherited trait born of the need to face adversity. They theorize that optimism was essential to perpetuate our species. These basic survival reasons have long since ceased to be paramount, but optimism persists as an integral part of

Things will get better?

our makeup. Often because of our most optimistic predictions, we are tremendously disappointed. "A man on the moon by 1955" and "A cure for cancer by 1960," are two statements made by knowledgeable men where the predictions were unfulfilled. Very few events, on the other hand, meet expectations. Most professional liability insurance underwriters put restrictive clauses in their policies of insurance coverage for excluding errors in cost estimates and failure to make timely delivery of plans. The reason? The optimistic evaluations of costs and schedules by design professionals frequently have been in error. In fact, the numbers of these errors have been so high and the impact on underwriting so great, that the exclusions became a protective necessity to some insurers.

Uncle Sam will not rescue you

What can a design professional in private practice do to cope with optimism so as to avert a claim or litigation when he makes cost or time estimations? Clearly, he may not expect the same sort of accommodation given by the U. S. Government to Lockheed on the C5A aircraft when they exceeded their estimate by billions of dollars. Rather, he should take steps to ascertain that cost and time estimates do not lead to his ruin. It calls for planning. In fact, the same careful planning that a design professional would devote to a system design should be applied to the preparation of cost estimates and time schedules.

Safety factors

In design work, it is quite common for the design professional to make computations and include a safety factor in order to deal with the unexpected. This is, in effect, a procedure to protect against optimism. The same technique may be his intended practice in cost estimating and scheduling. But is this safety factor allowance really part of his technique? Or does he subconsciously seek to encourage clients by providing optimistic cost estimates or time schedules?

Keep in mind that the claims brought against design professionals because of errors in estimates of costs or schedules have been so frequent that many underwriters consider them uninsurable. Think about your own practice. Or better than that, run a box score on your last year's work.

Exhibit 16 may assist you in evaluating your cost estimates. After you have entered your own data on these or similar forms, rate yourself. If you find that your cost estimates were exceeded by more than 10% on over 20% of your jobs, give yourself a **poor** rating. If you find that your cost estimates were exceeded on less than 20% of your projects, rate yourself **good**. A score where your cost estimates were not exceeded by more than a few percentage points should be rated **very good.**

Successful scheduling of design services is sometimes said to be more of an art than a science. The ability to predict a design schedule with any degree of consistency is rare. Yet, the practical, commercial world insists that you establish and follow some timetable. It is easier to follow a realistic schedule than an unduly optimistic one. Exhibit 17 may help you to determine how well your firm has been meeting project deadlines.

Among the many variables which influence the scheduling of design services, some can be anticipated and accounted for and some cannot. Some elements affecting progress of a design effort are beyond your control. For this reason, it is unadvisable for you to agree to be unconditionally obligated to delivery on time without regard to the reason for the delay. The more equitable contract documents between the client and the designer generally include a provision that the designer shall **not** be held answerable for damages caused by delays in his performance which arise out of events beyond his reasonable control. Remember that even if you are aware of this possible pitfall and guard against it by an appropriate contract provision, you are still faced with the possibility of delays occasioned by factors which **are** within your control and which must be evaluated in terms of manhours of effort within your firm.

At times you may be tempted to drastically cut your schedule at the urging of the client. Even if it means risking the loss of the project, you would be better advised to refuse a tight schedule than to wind up on litigation based upon your failure to make timely delivery or based upon the errors that have crept in.

Mapping the unknowns

123

EXHIBIT 16

COST ESTIMATE RATING

COST ESTIMATE
ACCURACY RATING

Time Period Covered: Jan. 1, 1979 to July 1, 1979

ACCURACY SCORE

No. Projects Estimated	No. Estimates Exceeded	% Rating
27	4	14.8%

PROJECTS ESTIMATED		FINAL COST ESTIMATE	BID FIGURE (or actual cost) (or contr. price)	PERCENTAGE OF ESTIMATE		REMARKS:
JOB NO.	NAME			−%	+%	
79-09	Able Office Bldg.	$416,820.	$404,240	−.03		Includes base bid plus alternates
79-06	Barnes Arcade	27,450.	31,400*		+15.0	*Bid = $39,600 Design modified
79-11	Craft Marina	164,290.	157,205	−.04		Includes increment No. 1A only
79-41	Dale Center	67,920.	62,780	−7.5		Cost per sq. ft. used at client request
79-26	Elgin Tower	1,897,640.	2,156,760		+13.4	*Not including owner furnished equip.
79-37	Foxworth Acres	787,140.	692,410	−12.1		Includes alternates accepted
79-46	Gains Clinic Bldg.	101,770.	97,890	−4.0		Base bid only

124

EXHIBIT 17

SCHEDULE RATING

PROJECT COMPLETION DATE — RATING

Time Period Covered: JAN. 1, 1979   to JULY 1, 1979

COMPLETION SCORE		
PROJECTS COMPLETED	DEADLINES EXCEEDED	% RATING
24	3	12.5 %

PROJECTS COMPLETED		FINAL DEADLINE DATE	DESIGN COMPLETION DATE	NO. OF DAYS		REMARKS:
JOB NO.	NAME			EARLY	LATE	
79-47	XENON BUILDING	JAN. 31	JAN. 30	1		DEADLINE EXTENDED
79-22	MIDTOWN COMPLEX	FEB. 14	FEB. 14	—	—	
79-04	100 MAIN ST. BLDG.	FEB. 20	FEB. 28		8	JOB CAPTAIN ILL FROM JAN. 6 TO JAN. 14

Impossible deadlines make E&O possible

A round-the-clock working to meet a deadline is well-known to produce fatigue which can reduce the efficiency level of even your most competent employees to the point where absurd errors creep into the drawings and specifications.

The vices of short deadlines are numerous. One illustrative situation involves a design professional faced with a deadline which is virtually impossible to meet. Reacting from extreme pressure from the client, the design professional issues incomplete drawings and specifications. This is followed by a desperate attempt to complete the design and communicate this information to the contractor by voluminous addenda before the bids are due. The addenda are not transmitted in sufficient time for the contractor to assemble an accurate bid figure. In order to cover the cost of contemplated additional work, the contractor is prone to submit a substantially larger bid figure than would otherwise be the case. The owner, as a result, may discover that the budget is exceeded at that stage or he may discover it at a later stage when the change orders occur. Expensive change orders may be the only way to correct the serious errors and omissions occuring as a result of the design professional not having had adequate time to conduct a careful check of the drawings and specifications.

Avoid slippage habits

Exceeding schedules from time to time is normal. But a pattern showing that you have failed to complete at least 80% of your projects on time should alert you to the fact that you are being unrealistic; you are too optimistic.

Many firms keep a running box score of their cost estimates and timeliness. It is a good idea. It is an excellent professional liability loss prevention technique. It will immediately demonstrate to you when you, or one of your project managers, allow optimism too free a rein. Before you agree to an unrealistic schedule, study the risks involved. By accepting only those projects where there is sufficient time to do a good job, you perceptibly reduce your exposure to professional liability claims.

Professional services are human services. Control of exposure to loss rests in influencing the behavioral attitudes of people in a manner which will lessen the probability of loss. This is particularly true of professional services where there is a large measure of subjective judgment involved; that is, cost estimating and time scheduling. It is a little difficult to convince a design professional in private practice that he is not doing everything possible to control this exposure, and that he must counsel his employees to "be careful." He understandably feels that he is in the best position to know the nuances and ramifications of his own design and how it will ultimately affect cost and time factors. Again, however, following past practices may not be adequate to stem the optimistic feelings that he might have concerning the cost of **his** design. In addition, he should be constantly aware that human attitudes have a large bearing on the success or failure of a professional in making a subjective evaluation on costs and time factors.

Some firms, recognizing the importance of this particular function in their professional services, control their optimistic attitudes by having persons other than the designer develop the cost estimates and schedules. The net result is to get an opinion that is independent from those most closely identified with the job.

Other firms simply have a second person check the designer's cost estimate computations and time factors. This second-person method leaves much to be desired, since the checker's responsibility is not the same as it would be when the checker himself determines an accurate cost figure and a realistic schedule.

Several Midwestern firms have reported that they hold conferences concerning cost estimates. The person who computes the figures is asked to explain his reasoning to the senior members of the firm. This puts a tremendous burden on the estimator, and makes him aware of the importance of this function. This also requires the leaders of the firm to be directly involved in the estimating procedures before the fur starts flying.

Human errors are here to stay

Check and double check

127

What about the one-man shop? If it is impossible to hold conferences and have different individuals compute the cost estimates, the best course to follow is the second look approach. We have all heard the adage, "Better sleep on it." A second look is a very good professional liability loss prevention technique.

Cost estimating and scheduling are, and will continue to be, prime sources of professional liability claims against the design profesional in private practice. He can do so much to mitigate the threat from this area by approaching these tasks as he would his design work and by including in his methodology a safety factor that is well-conceived.

Reach understanding

Regardless of your past success in predicting costs, the next time you are asked to make an estimate for a client, carefully review with him the purpose of your estimate. Take extraordinary care to explain to him the kind of information your estimate is intended to convey: a very general and approximate picture of the cost which he may take into consideration with other information in arriving at a preliminary budget for the project. Some design professionals also make an effort to tell their clients what the cost estimate is **not** intended to do. It is **not** a guaranteed maximum figure.

Your task is difficult. If you attempt to make your estimate accurate and realistic, you obviously run the risk that your estimate will be so low that the client may feel misled. If you "beef-up" your estimate to protect against this risk, and the actual cost turns out to be much lower, the client may get the impression you are careless with your estimating and thus may also be so in your designing. Your choice could be said to be the lesser of two evils. From the professional liability view, your best path is to be reasonably conservative in your estimating — particularly if the client is suspected of lacking an understanding of the purpose of your estimate. Remember that few design professionals have been sued because their cost estimates were too high. The same reasoning may be applied to schedules.

J. Collecting Your Fee

If you can count yourself among those design professionals whose clients pay you on time, you are extremely fortunate. A look at the Accounts Receivable file in many offices reveals a problem which defies solution. Although other professions have devised numerous tactics to deal with clients who do not pay on time, practicing design professionals usually lack the means to obtain prompt payment for their services. It is a situation obviously requiring tact. If you press too hard for payment, you may lose a client; if you delay, the client may continue to postpone payments.

A substantial number of professional liability claims within recent years involved consultants' attempts to collect their fees. A superficial examination of these claims may indicate that the suit against the design professional originated from an alleged error or omission. A more penetrating investigation presents the following picture.

The design professional performs professional services in accordance with the agreement and the client appears satisfied with the result. After repeated billing for his fee, the consultant discovers the first evidence of dissatisfaction by the client. After a lengthy wait for payment of his fee, the consultant finds that as he becomes more insistent, his client becomes more dissatisfied. When the client becomes aware of the consultant's intention to sue for payment, the client **then** claims that the consultant is professionally incompetent. The design professional institutes a suit to collect a fee of, say, $10,000. At that time, a countersuit is brought by the client alleging professional negligence and asking for damages amounting to $500,000.

To businessmen wise in the commercial world, this tactic by a client is recognized as one of the oldest ploys used to avoid payment for services rendered. However, the practicing design professional, untutored in the realities of business life and with his reputation at stake, is peculiarly vulnerable to a client who chooses this seemingly unethical practice. Only a few years ago, this situation was rare. Today,

Design professionals lack the ability to obtain prompt payment for their services

The root of all evil

the increasing frequency of this type of claim is symptomatic of the design professionals' inability to cope with it effectively.

What can be done? In an effort to discourage this type of client reaction, some design professionals have adopted a method of obtaining written evidence of a client's satisfaction with his performance while relations are still relatively harmonious between them. As a routine matter, they secure a Completion Statement from the client as soon after completion of the project as possible. One form of Completion Statement is shown in Exhibit 18.

The Completion Statement: a defense against claims

EXHIBIT 18

COMPLETION STATEMENT
X Y Z, Inc.

The design professional, _____

has performed the design services, including construction review, in accordance with the agreement dated _____

with the Client, _____,

in a manner acceptable to the Client, except as may be noted below.

(Space for list of exceptions, if any)

_____   _____
Design Professional's Signature   Client's Signature

                            _____
                                   Date

You said it

Although the Completion Statement is not an absolute deterrent to a subsequent lawsuit involving collection of fee, it acts as a reasonable business precaution and may tend to dissuade a client from basing a lawsuit on allegations of professional negligence which have little or no merit.

Some owners may resist payment only for good and sufficient reasons. Others have a standard policy of postponing payment until they are threatened with legal action. Your awareness of some of the predictable human responses in common business situations can go far in stemming the present tide of this type of professional liability claim.

Finally, the manner in which you request payment of a delinquent debt has a great deal to do with the likelihood of prompt payment. Your attorney may be familiar with methods of eliciting favorable reaction from a problem client. By asking his advice **before** you write to a client who owes you money, you may avoid unnecessary litigation and at the same time obtain more successful results than you might otherwise expect.

K. Arbitration as a Sole and Exclusive Remedy

An easy out?

It is becoming increasingly popular to have an arbitration clause in contracts where construction is involved. This is no less true of the contract of hire the design professional signs than it is with other parties to the performance of the work. There is a theory that has been widely promulgated which says that compared to the legal process, arbitration is somehow less costly, more efficient, and produces greater equity in disputes involving parties to construction. The truth of this remains in question. In fact, in some instances there have been arbitration proceedings which seem to go directly contrary to those popular suppositions.

Arbitration may be quite satisfactory in some circumstances and in some jurisdictions, but it also has its drawbacks. Therefore, do not blithely sign a contract containing a clause which makes arbitration the sole and exclusive remedy for any dispute arising out of your performance of professional services. If you do, you may cause yourself serious trouble.

An arbitration clause is an agreement between you and another party requiring you to perform in a certain manner following a contingent happening (that is, any matter giving rise to a dispute). How can your agreement with one party affect a third party not participating in the contract? In some jurisdictions, it may not affect them at all. Why is this of concern to you? One of the main reasons is that your professional liability insurance underwriter may be that third party who is not a party to the contract and who will not want to participate in arbitration as a method of establishing your legal liability in the event of loss. If this is the case, your underwriter might, in some jurisdictions, successfully argue that an arbitration proceeding which holds against you has no effect upon the underwriter's legal liability and that you have violated the terms and conditions of your policy of insurance by submitting to arbitration without prior approval.

Just get the facts

Of even greater concern might be the third party who is critical to your defense in a professional liability claim who is not in privity of contract with you or your client. This means that if you sign a contract of hire in which arbitration is made the sole and exclusive remedy, you may be unable to draw upon that person who is your best defense for aid. Supposing you specify a type of material or a component and it fails. If your client insists upon arbitration and you have no means of drawing in the manufacturer or supplier of the failed article, you will be in a poor position.

Another problem with arbitration as the sole and exclusive remedy where professional liability is concerned is your inability to conduct discovery proceedings. While in a court of law you can examine your adversaries' files, this is not always possible in arbitration. How then do you defend yourself when all of the cards may be held by your adversary and they have them covered up? It may be difficult.

While many states have effective arbitration laws that make it binding on the parties, this is not universally so. This is another item which you should carefully examine before agreeing to arbitration as the sole and exclusive remedy in the event of a dispute. It may not be enforceable in your jurisdiction.

One shortcoming that can be particularly critical if you are dealing with complicated technical matters is that in an arbitration proceeding, either party may enter any type of evidence that they see fit. This sometimes leads to a snowstorm of irrelevant data that so thoroughly confuses the arbitrators that justice is difficult to discern and compromise seems to be the easy way out.

Another point to consider is that arbitration is not subject to appeal in most jurisdictions. Some of the landmark cases that have been most helpful to design professionals in private practice have been resolved upon appeal. In the absence of appeal, precedents cannot be set which may later be used to defend other design professionals.

No recourse

For the above reasons, it would be well for you to consult with your insurance broker and attorney before signing a contract which makes arbitration the sole and exclusive remedy. Inquiries of your fellow consultants about their experiences in arbitration proceedings may show that there is as much dissatisfaction with this mode of dispute handling as with courtroom procedure. If you believe it to be a good method of resolving differences of opinion, make certain that you give your underwriter the opportunity of agreeing to an arbitration provision prior to your involvement. Many underwriters readily accept this method of settlement; others feel that it is more expensive, takes longer and produces less equity. Their belief in this regard could have a bearing on the effectiveness of your coverage.

L. Your Recruiting Practices

It may seem ironic, but the most important asset of your firm is not listed on the financial balance sheet. We refer to the creative, competent, and hard-working personnel on your staff. Your hiring procedures of today will play a big part in your professional future, for the competence of those you will hire tomorrow, next week, or next year will have as much effect upon your continued success as do those presently in your employ. With so much at stake the pity is that more is not known about evaluating prospective personnel during the recruiting process.

The human asset

The present methods of evaluating personnel used by most design professionals are somewhat primitive. These methods usually require the filling out of an application form or submission of a resume and one or two interviews with one or more principals of the firm. Yet the desirable characteristics in the areas of intellectual capacity, social adaptability, drive, creativity, and personal interest do not reveal themselves on an application form. The psychological and intelligence tests, which at one time were employed by many firms, today are prohibited by law unless it can be shown conclusively that they relate directly to job performance. The burden of proof that such a relationship exists rests on the employer. For this reason, such tests have all but disappeared as a viable technique for selecting personnel.

1. Exploding Some Myths

At about the turn of the century, the notion grew that human behavior could be measured and forecasted. Since then, hundreds of batteries of tests have been devised, texts written, seminars conducted, and theories propounded. Much of this was anecdotal in nature and not supported by hard data. As a result, a body of conventional wisdom has evolved that recent data-based research has found to be just about useless. Some examples will serve to underline the point:

In 1931, actuaries employed by the august Metropolitan Life Insurance Company published the first of a series of results that indicated some people are accident prone.[5] If you were to question the average employer today, chances are, he would concur. The results of the Metropolitan analysis and subsequent texts written by psychologists and others have permeated the conventional wisdom. Modern statistical techniques, however, cast a pall on this theory. Jean Surry, a Canadian researcher, summarizes the results as follows:

---

[5]Preventing Taxicab Accidents. Metropolitan Life Insurance Company, 1931.

"Prones," whether they exist or not, at most represent a very *small number* of the repeaters. They are a fourth order term: the vast majority are a victim of "chance"; some suffer higher risk exposure due to the environment; a few represent unequal personal liability, e.g., the very young or old, the inexperienced, etc.; and the prones would be the smallest term of all.[6]

The myth that college grades or position in graduating class serves as a predictor of adult achievement was put to rest by Professor Albert Shapero, as follows:

Now there is little evidence that shows that GRADES have a significant relationship to subsequent performance on the job, despite many studies that attempted to find such a relationship. Such efforts have included studies of engineering school graduates, scientists and engineers in governmental laboratories and in private industry, nursing school graduates, full-time praticing physicians, MBA graduates from various business schools, public school teachers, college graduates in general, and foreign students. The preponderance of evidence comes down heavily in support of the conclusion that *there is no relationship between grades and job performance*. One study even found a negative correlationship between grades and the rated creativity of practicing scientists. Oh yes! There is one study of scientists and engineers in a government laboratory that shows a correlation. It shows that those with the highest performance ratings came from the second and third quartiles of their college classes. There is also a study of MBA graduates from a top-ranked college that shows a mild positive correlationship

[6]Surry, Jean. Industrial Accident Research: A Human Engineering Appraisal. Department of Labor, Labor Safety Council, Toronto, Canada. 1971. p. 167.

between grades made *in elective courses* and subsequent salaries.[7]

Should you doubt Shapero's words, you may wish to follow the steps of one of his Ph.D. candidates who produced a four and one-half page bibliography on the subject. She explained her motivation and results as follows:

> I just didn't believe it. After nearly a quarter century, 4/5's of my life, chasing the 4.00's, 95's, A+'s, and E's dispensed by my various schools, I had too much at stake to accept at face value the ravings of an iconoclastic, slightly eccentric professor, no matter how charming he might be.
>
> . . . So I smugly decided to check "the data" myself. I was certain that Shapero was mistaken. If he wasn't, I needed to do some hard thinking.
>
> He wasn't.[8]

A final myth concerned with the hiring of new personnel is the value of the interview as a screening device. Surveys have indicated that this is the selection tool most relied upon by employers. Research employing hard data, however, reveals the interview has limited value as a selection tool. Martin, Kearney, and Holdefer conclude:

> Our findings concerning the hiring impact of the interview are especially disconcerting when coupled with other well-known and documented research findings . . . Most important of these, the low validity and reliability of the interview. Based on our work, we would like to concur (as have others) with the futile advice of England and Paterson given ten years ago:

---

[7] The Manager: The Decision to Hire. CHEMTECH, February, 1977. p. 70.

[8] Ibid.

With full recognition of the improbability of the acceptance of our advice, we would like to suggest a moratorium on books, articles and other writings about "how to interview," "do's and don'ts" about interviewing and the like, until there is sufficient research evidence about the reliability and validity of the interview as an assessment device to warrant its use.[9]

2. Some Recruiting Criteria

One factor that has inhibited the development of hiring criteria is the lack of objective data. This seems to have been overcome in a study conducted by Stanford Research Institute.[10]

The data for this information came from the records (with names deleted) of 35,000 scientists and engineers. These were cooperatively supplied by 22 aerospace-defense firms in the Boston and Los Angeles areas. About ten percent of these records were for employees who had left the company so that differences could be detected between the characteristics of these terminated engineers and scientists and those still employed. In addition, a record of about 3,300 scientists and engineers and 2,000 other salaried employees in the Denver, Tucson, and Orlando areas was available from a previous study made for the Department of Defense on the mobility of R&D workers.

The study focused on factors relating to the individual — not the company-individual relationship

[9] Martin, D. D., Kearney, W. J., and Holdefer, G. D. The Decision to Hire: A Comparison of Selected Tools. University of Cincinnati, Reprint Series No. 45, 1976.

[10] Howell, Richard P. "Engineers on the Move," Engineering Manpower Bulletin, No. 11, Engineering Manpower Commission of Engineers Joint Council, New York. June, 1968.

— that affect the turnover rate. Fourteen hiring criteria were derived.[11]

- In hiring a new employee, take advantage of the available, qualified, local applicants. If local applicants are not available, hire along migratory streams: this includes the migration from the less urban areas to the more urban areas, as well as the well-established paths east to west and south to north, except from the north to Florida. If you are hiring in an area outside the path of the migratory stream, hire a returnee or one whose wife is a returnee.

- Turnover may be reduced by hiring only the person well-qualified by his special educational background. However, there may be some danger in hiring an over-qualified person.

- The older the applicant (up to age 57), the less likely he is to resign.

- The fewer the number of prior full-time jobs an applicant has held, the longer the period he might be expected to remain with your organization — at least up to the level of eight prior jobs.

- The more an applicant knows of your operation and feels compatible with this operation, either through his unique interest and knowledge or on advice of friends and acquaintances, the more likely he will remain with your organization.

- Effectiveness increases with age up to about age 50.

- Effectiveness increases with level of education.

---

[11] Some of the criteria listed may now be prohibited by law.

- The applicant manifesting ambition as his primary motivation tends to be a more effective employee.

- The applicant who worked in a company similar to, or associated with, your company tends to be more effective than another.

Parallel experience

- The married applicant seems more effective, on the average, than the single person who, in turn, is more effective than the divorced or separated person.

- The applicant with the experience of three prior, full-time positions is more effective than one from any other category. One who has had no prior position or who has held more than eight positions is less effective.

- The applicant who has received his degree from a school demanding high entrance requirements tends to be more effective than one from another college or university.

- An applicant who has a history of salary levels or salary increases excelling others of similar background has been evaluated by his earlier employers as a more effective employee than those whose range has been below average.

One criterion stood out above all others in the Stanford Research Institute analysis.

- Persons who were hired after being introduced to the company through acquaintances did much better, on the average, and were less likely to resign than those hired through other avenues.

The best screen

Although those that were hired in response to ads in journals did quite well, those that responded to newspaper advertisements did not perform up to average, and those that were hired through placement agencies did the poorest of all.

139

M. Motivating Your Personnel

Similar to the state of knowledge regarding interviewing, the data-based theories covering motivation are sparse. One thing is starkly plain, however. Production differences are great between individuals. Harvard's William James found that hourly employees could coast along at only 20-30 percent of their ability and not be fired. He found that highly motivated employees produce at about 80-90 percent of their abilities — 2½ to 4½ times greater.[12]

William Shockley found the difference between technical professionals could be greater still — the exceptional outproduced the average by a margin greater than ten to one.[13]

The jury is still out regarding what motivates people. It is becoming clear, however, that job pressure is not bad. In fact, healthy people seem to need to experience stress and, once a challenge is met, search for new stresses.

Based on data obtained from 22 research laboratories, Hall and Lawler[14] identified three main types of pressures that design professionals face — time, quality, and financial responsibility. Using a variety of measures, Hall and Lawler found:

> In marked contrast to the dark view of job pressure presented in many writings, we see that certain pressures are definitely functional in the laboratories we studied. Quality pressure was particularly useful, being related positively to both the job involvement of the individual professionals and the technical effectiveness of their

---

[12] Hersey, Paul and Kenneth H. Blanchard, *Management of Organizational Behavior*, Prentice-Hall, Inc., Englewood Cliffs, NJ, 1972. p. 5.

[13] Proceedings of IRE, 1967. p. 283.

[14] Hall, Douglas T. and Edward E. Lawler, "Job Pressure and Research Performance," *Current Trends in Psychology*, Irving L. Janis, ed., William Kaufmann, Inc., Los Altos, CA, 1977. pp. 291-300.

legal entanglements caused by imperfections and simultaneously make these individuals useful and productive, it is first necessary to recognize their strong and weak points. A means must then be devised to eliminate or compensate for the weaknesses.

To illustrate this point, let us refer to the experience of one design professional firm which employed a particular project engineer with a strong academic background and many years of experience. After several weeks of trial his performance appeared to justify the decision to hire him. He showed a capacity for wise engineering judgment, an ability to make sensible systems selection for various applications, and a wide knowledge of available, good-quality equipment, plus the advantages and disadvantages of each. He had the capacity to assemble and write a complete specification, he deftly fielded complex questions in a pressure atmosphere, and he displayed good working relationships with the men he supervised as well as his superiors. All in all, this engineer gave the impression of having above average competence in all areas necessary to produce a high quality design with a minimum of errors.

Within a couple of months, the initial evaluation had to be revised. The firm's checking procedures fortunately included a careful review of the initial design calculations performed by every project engineer. Review was routinely conducted by the department head approximately 75% of the way through the project design. The newly hired project engineer, a mechanical engineer, had committed a number of elementary arithmetical errors of the type which would not usually be caught in a computer check. This disconcerting discovery necessitated a complete redesign of the project, which involved air conditioning equipment. The calculations of this project engineer were quickly corrected, but when the new and the former results were compared, it was clear that a substantial increase in the output of the air conditioning equipment was necessary. Larger equipment was required which would be capable of the increased performance. It was then mandatory that additional space be allotted in the building for the air

Overcome mental handicaps

conditioning equipment. Virtually every drawing had to be redone. The client was most unhappy at the prospects of a delay.

An examination of the type of arithmetical error that was made indicated a serious flaw in the project engineer's ability. He was unable to sense when the order of magnitude of a particular number was out of proportion to the size of the system. For example, if various sources of heat gain on an air conditioning system should correctly total 800,000 BTU per hour, and through some error the total reads only 80,000 BTU per hour, any competent, experienced engineer should immediately sense an error. The mistake was blatantly evident, for some individual numbers contributing to the total exceeded the 80,000 figure by themselves. He repeated this type of error several times throughout his calculations. Making detection doubly difficult was the fact that one error often compensated for another; that is, the error in magnitude in one case would **exceed** the correct total and in another case be **less than** the correct total.

After the problem was discovered, the principals conducted a private conference attended by the somewhat shaken engineer. They pointed out to him his errors and the extra work which resulted. He admitted that a tendency to make this type of error had plagued him continuously during his career, yet he had not been able to master it. The short-term solution to the problem was quite simple. On each project assigned to him thereafter, all calculations were performed and checked by other engineers.

The long-term solution to the problem included periodic intensive training sessions, specifically designed to cultivate in that engineer the habit of routinely checking the order of magnitude of the answer obtained against that which was expected. He was taught a simple yet effective means to accurately locate the decimal point. A fundamental gap in this engineer's training was at last filled; however, it almost led to a costly claim against the firm. The client,

The feel for right or wrong

Continuing education

144

through some accommodation, was in this case able to bear the burden of delay.

After several months, the project engineer was permitted to do limited calculations in low-risk areas which were then carefully checked. Once the project engineer was aware of the importance the firm attached to this, his performance improved considerably.

A valuable lesson can be learned from this episode by every design professional who supervises any personnel employed to do design calculations. First, establish a performance rating system to periodically evaluate the performance of each person. Assemble a checklist with as many categories as are appropriate, such as mathematical accuracy, legibility of calculations, letter writing ability, and similar characteristics important to a design professional. (See Exhibit 19.)

A systematic approach to employee errors

In many cases a particular project can be broken into various stages of completion and represented in successive columns on a performance evaluation form. These could be labeled, for example, "Schematic Design Phase," "Design Development Phase," "Construction Documents Phase," and "Construction Review Phase." This would permit evaluation of performance at various stages of a project. It is not reasonable to expect that haphazard detection methods can be used successfully to reveal haphazard performance. A systematic approach in helping your technical personnel to overcome bad practices can substantially reduce the number of mistakes and delays.

P. Moonlighting Employees

Do any of your employees work for other firms or individuals on projects that are even vaguely similar to

EXHIBIT 19

EMPLOYEE PERFORMANCE EVALUATION
CHECKLIST
X Y Z, Inc.

Evaluation By Richard Roe   Date 1/79 to 1/80

Name of Employee John Guideline   Title Draftsman

P — Poor	F — Fair	E — Excellent
A — Barely Adequate	G — Good	* — Not Applicable

		JAN	FEB	MAR	APR	MAY	JUNE	JULY	AUG	SEPT	OCT	NOV	DEC
1.	Mathematical Accuracy	A											
2.	Ability to Follow Directions	F											
3.	Quality of Lettering	G											
4.	Quality of Writing	E											
5.	Legibility of Calculations	G											
6.	Blueprint Reading Ability	G											
7.	Drafting Ability General	E											
8.	Care Exercised in Filing	G											
9.	Letter Writing & Composition	*											
10.	Language Usage and Vocabulary	F											
11.	Telephone Courtesy & Manner	*											
12.	Capacity to Supervise	*											
13.	Relations with Supervisors	E											
14.	Relations with Subordinates	*											
15.	Engineering Judgment	F											
16.	Initiative	G											
17.	Housekeeping	G											

REMARKS

John is not now performing at a level requiring him to write letters, use the telephone or supervise others. At present he does simple calculations only.

those they do for you? If so, your professional liability exposures may be affected. Because of the fluctuating nature of project work in some firms, this activity may be widespread and actually condoned by a few employers. However, it can be hazardous to the financial health of both the employee and his employer.

Why do employees moonlight? There are usually several reasons given, foremost of which is the financial gain — the needed supplement to the basic income. This reason is closely followed by the rationale that the project or work is so minor that no one else, especially an established, reputable firm would touch it. Both of these justifications spell trouble.

Employees who solicit outside work, almost without exception, carry no professional liability insurance. They are often unaware of the legal risks to themselves and they **and** their employers are unaware of all risks to the employer. The risks to the employer from possible deterioration in the quality and amount of work a moonlighting employee performs during the regular working day are generally recognized risks; however, the claim made by plaintiffs that the employer derives benefit from the employee's moonlighting, since he would not otherwise be able to afford the employee, is not a generally recognized risk.

Psychologists contend that the average individual is capable of a limited quantum of productivity in any given time span. If this productive effort is expended at times and in directions other than regular employment, the employer is deprived of benefit. In addition, intense and concentrated output is a drain on one's endurance. Although an afterhours change of pace can be refreshing, even if the effort is immense, the energy required to continue with the same type of output in outside activities as expended in the office is tremendously high. Fatigue results and hence the probability of mistakes skyrockets.

Since most projects that invite moonlighting are by their very nature speculative and with a limited budget, the possibility of litigation is extremely high. If litigation does occur, the limited financial reserves of the moonlighting employee can mean the loss of his assets. Even if the employer is not a party to the litigation, the firm suffers from the mental and emotional anxiety of the moonlighting employee.

One alternate to moonlighting is to interest the employee in taking a more active part in the management of the firm. This, of course, has to be both desired by the employee, and desirable from the firm's viewpoint. Employees who are encouraged to increase their level of participation in the affairs of the firm are more likely to channel their energies in the directions beneficial to the firm. Considering the professional liability aspects, the stipulation that employees do not moonlight is not only desirable, it is a *NECESSITY*.

An example of the employer being a party to the litigation is the case of a moonlighter who did a favor for a neighbor. The neighbor wanted to make a room out of the garage and build a new garage. The new garage required retaining walls along the driveway. The employee (a structural engineer) designed the retaining walls for $50. The neighbor got another friend to do the contracting. The backfill of the walls subsequently settled, causing cracks in the old garage and the driveway to the new garage. During a party a guest tripped over the cracks in the driveway and broke a leg. The neighbor sued the contractor, the moonlighter, and both their employers since neither of the former had any money.

Moonlighting employees are a possible professional liability.

Q. The Risks of New Relationships

New relationships involve both employees and new partners. Either may bring with him, along with marvelous traits of competency in technical matters, in supervisory capacities, and in dealing with clientele, some not-so-marvelous liabilities.

Employees can be agents, that is "one who acts for, or in the place of, another by authority from him."

However, every partner in a firm is an agent of his firm for the purpose of its business. His acts bind the partnership of which he is a member unless he has no authority to act for them in that particular matter. **In addition, the person with whom he is dealing must be aware of the fact that he has no authority.**

If after establishing his new relationship with you, a person completes a project for himself or his previous firm, another person can argue that he was your agent. This is particularly true if he **IS** concurrently an agent for you on a similar project.

R. Decision-Making and Professional Liability

The menace of professional liability attack haunts every design professional. The roots of costly, time-consuming suits lurk everywhere. But man, a creature of habit, tends to cling to his familiar way of doing things; the application of habitual, automatic responses to recurrent situations is economical. Freed from appraising and reappraising the same problem, formulating and reformulating the same solution, the professional can grapple with the new and exciting challenges. But that same habit tends to dull his perception. Once comfortably ingrained, habits tend to blind people to changes in conditions.

A design professional who predicates his business decisions upon the experience he accumulated years ago is courting ruin. He must confront the ugly fact that his professional liability has become a potential windfall for callous or uninformed individuals hoping to recoup their losses or even make gains at another person's expense. The peril of the burgeoning trend to victimize design professionals makes it imperative that the whole process of decision-making be re-evaluated.

As a decision maker, the design professional is unique. The problems he deals with and his approach to them are vastly different from those of a banker, a stockbroker, or an admiral. His orientation and the nature of his task require that he allot his energies to his duties in order of importance. His success and satisfaction are born of his willingness to accept design (as opposed to business) risks. A design professional does not try to deal in absolutes; rather, by measuring his design concept against probabilities, he develops a high tolerance to uncertainties. With his objective always in mind, he wrests answers from the available alternatives. He thinks in terms of how it can be done, rather than why it cannot be done.

The voice which says to him "Go to it," in his decision-making process should, in many instances, be saying "Stop." Too often the design professional draws the analogy that the same decision-making process that applies to his design tasks can be applied, with equal success, to the business aspects of his private practice. When confronted with essentially a business problem, the design professional does not hesitate to take the risk; rather, he plunges ahead, certain that, like the design problem, it is solvable. At this point he exposes himself to extensive professional liability jeopardy.

How can an organization's management personnel be trained to perceive those decisions which will avert professional liability difficulties? Are there management axioms which design professionals can apply to their business judgment which will keep them relatively free from the threat of professional liability claims? In order to answer these questions, there must be some understanding of decision-making as a business process.

1. Formalized Decision-Making

A great deal has been written on the subject of structuring an organization in a manner that will facilitate the making of important business decisions on a formal basis. Usually this involves the use of a matrix or a graph so that the shape of a decision can be examined. The positive features of a project are listed on one side of the graph, and the negative ones on the other. Various weights are assigned to items connected with the work to be performed. Ideally speaking, those jobs which show the highest degree of positive response are the jobs that a firm should accept. It's that simple.

The trouble is that each positive or negative factor must be weighted, and values are usually assigned by judgment. If professional liability is interjected as a consideration, values change. While it is true that business reasons for positively examining a piece of work frequently coincide with professional liability considerations, technical values may be antithetical.

Judgment?
Or guesses?

Design professionals are born risk-takers. The risks they assume are not business risks but technical risks. This creates an enigma in the decision-making process. To formalize decision-making by the production of a graph merely points out the conflict which may exist between the business decision and the technical decision. In the final analysis, judgmental evaluations must be based on experience. (When the executive officers of some of the major U. S. corporations were asked how they made their decisions, they frequently responded that they made them "by intuition." It would be consoling to think that they made them through the manipulation of a highly structured thought process. Obviously this was not the case.)

2. What Then?

If a design professional cannot rely upon a formalized approach to decision-making in order to reduce the exposure to professional liability claims, what can he do? The answer is multiple.

One recommended procedure is to use ready-made guides and references to remind him of areas of exposure. Whatever process he uses in his decision-making, it should be flavored with the knowledge that professional liability risk is more prevalent in some areas than in others.

A second technique the design professional may apply in decision-making is frequently referred to as brain-storming. This technique is used by some consultants to evaluate the business aspects of work they are asked to do. Two groups of people who will be involved in projects sit on opposite

Your guess plus my
guess is better than
mine alone

sides of the table. One group presents all of the positive factors they can think of about the job; the other group presents the negative factors. A general harangue is the result, from which emerges decisions on matters of profit, professional liability exposure, and so on. This committee approach to decision-making has enjoyed some success, but also has its flaws (the influence of a dominant personality being only one of many). The Delphi technique, which requires independent responses through a third person, may overcome some of the objections to this approach.

3. An Expert

Perhaps the most successful of all decision-making methods — one that has had the greatest impact on professional liability claims as well as on business success — is the employment of trained managers. This was one of the techniques used by the industrialists to implement the fantastic rise of the United States to an economic power in the world. Even today, one often finds the management of great industrial complexes weighted heavily on the business side while the production people make up a relatively small portion of the management staff. This combination of production plus business talent created an extremely efficient team skilled at answering needs as they arose. Its impact on industry has been phenomenal!

By studying business history, the importance of strength in the makeup of the business manager can easily be seen. Many businesses that were dominated by technical or production-oriented people have failed. Those who permitted the business managers to operate on a level of acceptance equal or superior to technical and productive personnel have succeeded. Remember that the successful business entity is a multiphasal unit. All phases must be in balance if that unit is to remain stable. The design professional who emphasizes the design aspects over the business considerations of his practice is not running a well-balanced business unit. His decision-making process will be unduly influenced by design factors; these should be counterbalanced by business considerations. Ideally, this would accomplish two things:

- Increase productivity and service; and,

- Reduce the probability of professional liability claims.

What of the design professional firm that is too small to afford a full-time business manager? Some design professional firms are so constituted that principals must double in brass. The principals may manage personnel, accounting, production of new business, attend professional society meetings, and, on occasion, sweep the premises. Each task they try to do well. Most expertise in various fields is self-taught. That fact provides the clue for what must be done in order to apply modern business techniques to decision-making.

In those firms where income does not justify full-time business managers, the principals should expend some effort in an endeavor to train themselves in modern business methods. This takes some doing, for time is a short commodity. Yet, if professional liability claims are to be curbed, time must be spent in developing business skills to reinforce the knowledge necessary for making non-claims-producing decisions.

One further technique that may be used by the small design professional firm as a method of improving business decision-making is the group employment of a business manager. This experiment currently is being conducted by some firms. This entails an agreement among several consultants (usually multidisciplinary) to hire a full-time business manager who prorates his time among those in the group. Again, it is important that the weight of his judgment be accorded full acceptance. This, of course, means that the calibre of the individual and his management skills are of the utmost importance.

Alternatives while reaching critical mass

Group approach

153

There are several organizations which may provide help to a small businessman in the development of his management skills. The American Management Association is one. In addition, most of the major universities offer continuing education in the field of business.

IV
technical
procedures

IV
technical
procedures

Success in many professions depends largely upon the work done by those who have gone before. A handbook compiled by your predecessors is a great asset. Someone recognized the need for checking aids or sources of information which would make the work easier and faster with fewer errors. The use of procedural aids in achieving technical accuracy is not new. What is new is the use of these aids in the reduction of your professional liability exposure. The design activities which are highly susceptible to claims of this type are drawings, specification writing, and shop drawing review. These danger areas are given special treatment in subsequent pages.

A. Specifications Omissions and Ambiguities

One persistent source of professional liability claims is specifications. The designer's world-renowned penchant for precision and clarity is rarely exhibited in the written description of design. In truth, the average design professional is poorly prepared when it comes to the communication arts.

Anyone who studies a foreign language finds that the use of a dictionary to translate and define the meaning of words is essential if that particular language is to be learned. To those outside the construction industry, and to many within it, the words that designers use in a specification are a kind of special language. It is sensible to provide a brief dictionary to aid those who must understand exactly what the specifications mean. This may be done by a "Definitions" section in every specification. Define all words which have a special meaning or connote more than one meaning.

Many designers consider specification writing a thorn in their sides. This attitude is understandable when you consider that calculations and drawings are fundamentally design activities, but the written description of what is visually expressed on the drawings is a step removed from design activities. Effective specification writing requires special talents. Superficial treatment of specification writing can easily lead to the omission of an item critical to the successful completion of the project.

The specification checklist

One very successful method of avoiding specification omissions is through the specification checklist. This simply consists of a list of all specification provisions or categories and in appearance is similar to a specification index but with one important difference. The checklist contains every possible provision applicable to a particular design specialty. No actual specification for a particular project would contain every provision included in the checklist. The use of the specification checklist makes it unlikely that you would intentionally omit a pertinent or required provision. (Exhibit 20 illustrates one specification checklist applicable to general provisions.)

Many design professional offices have meticulously assembled their own checklists. Some mechanical and electrical consulting engineers have formulated one checklist of general provisions uniformly applicable to the electrical, heating, ventilating and air conditioning, plumbing, and fire protection specifica-

EXHIBIT 20

SPECIFICATION CHECKLIST
X Y Z Inc.
Mechanical and Electrical
Consulting Engineers
GENERAL PROVISIONS

Provision	Elec.	HV&AC	Plumb.	Fire Protec.
General		✓		
Scope of Work		✓		
Work not Included in this Contract		✓		
Work & Equipment by Owner		✓		
Drawings & Measurements: Accuracy of Data, Intent of Drawings and Specifications		✓		
Codes, Rules & Safety Orders		✓		
Licenses, Permits, Fees and Inspections		✓		
Manufacturer's Instructions		✓		
Shop Drawings and Construction Review		✓		
Material Lists and Substitutions		✓		
Coordination and Cooperation		✓		
Workmanship		✓		
Protection of Equipment		✓		
Demolition and Removal		✓		
Fire Prevention		✓		

Cutting and Patching	✓		
Damage to Premises	✓		
Restoration	NOT REQ'D		
Temporary Facilities	✓		
Preliminary Operations	✓		
New and Existing Services	MODIFIED		
Service Interruption, Modifications & Connections to Existing Utilities	NOT REQ'D.		
Storage of Tools and Equipment	✓		
Examination of Site	✓		
Examination and Backfill	✓		
Review of Installation before Covering	✓		
Adjustments	✓		
Cleaning of Equipment and Premises	✓		
Contractor's Guarantee	✓		
Definitions	✓		

tion sections. This is supplemented by material and equipment checklists peculiar to each individual section. Several civil engineering firms utilize this method when assembling specifications for underground utilities. In order to reduce the length of an extremely comprehensive material and equipment checklist, some design professional firms assemble several checklists, each one specially applicable to a particular type of method, system or project. One structural engineering firm assembled checklists for various types of structural systems by using building codes as a beginning point. This approach provided an additional benefit in that a more comprehensive knowledge of the contents of various codes naturally followed. The same idea can be used in the preparation of soil reports. Regardless of how you assemble your checklist, this device can be an invaluable aid in making your specification or report complete.

B. Drawing Omissions

The best means of communication with the contractor and his workmen is by your drawings. It follows that, above all, the drawings must be as complete and error-free as possible. Most design professionals carefully review the drawings and check the calculations for accuracy; review the materials specified, to make sure they fit the application; and eliminate conflicts between the specifications and the drawings. These checking methods are commonplace. Yet, major errors or omissions continue to occur. How do some design professional firms avoid this trouble? Those firms with good claims records attribute their freedom from trouble to the use of all the usual checking methods mentioned plus the following:

- design manuals (or in geotechnical engineering, procedure manuals), and

- design checklists.

The **design manual** is a step-by-step written description of all design methods to be followed in a specific type of system. General information about a particular type of system or method is found in handbooks. The design manual begins where the handbook leaves off. It serves as a more detailed guide. It reflects the special preferences of the firm. Some firms, after many years of experience, have rejected certain ideas as unacceptable or less desirable than others. The firm's design manual reflects these judgments. It could be termed the technical office policy.

The design manual

Your firm can formulate design manuals by having one or more of your best people outline the latest procedures used by your company in designing a system or method. After the outline is reviewed and approved by the principals of the firm, the manual can be committed to writing. You may wish to include standard calculation forms and samples of actual calculations performed on a project. The end of the manual can be reserved for special notes. When the manual is completed and in use, each project manager makes note of any design improvements or especially helpful information gained through experience. The notes are then typewritten, inserted into the back of the manual, and become part of it. Thus, the benefits of experience are passed to the next user of the manual.

Items peculiar to each project but of minor importance are not necessarily listed in the manual. Usually only those items or procedures repeatedly encountered on any project where this particular design is used are included. (See Exhibit 21 for a sample page of a design manual.)

EXHIBIT 21

X Y Z Inc.

AIR CONDITIONING

B. CHILLED WATER COOLING AND SPRAYED COIL AND SINGLE DUCT, LOW VELOCITY, HOT WATER REHEAT SYSTEM (Cont.)

   3. **Counterflow Piping Connections — Hot Water Coils**

      a. **Always** design the hot water piping connections to hot water reheat coils to produce **counterflow** between the air and water; the entering hot water connection **must** be on the leaving air side of the coil, and the leaving hot water connection **must** be on the entering air side of the coil.

      b. It is preferred that the leaving water connection be located at a higher elevation than the entering water connection to facilitate air bubble elimination, but this design consideration is **not** as important as having counterflow connections.

4. **Piping and Connections — Hot Water Coils**

   a. Detail the piping connections to a typical hot water reheat coil **only once** on the drawings. Each exception to the typical detail must be reviewed individually by requiring submittal of shop drawings for review.

   b. The standard typical isometric detail of piping connections to a horizontal air flow hot water reheat coil was carefully designed to provide the minimum number of joints in piping and fittings and still provide sufficient means of expansion and contraction in the piping. **Use This Detail!** Do **not** attempt to design one yourself without first checking with your supervisor.

   c. All hot water reheat coil piping accessories, such as thermometer wells, shut off and balancing values, etc., are shown on standard typical detail of hot water reheat coil No. HC-IX.

5. **Selection of Hot Water Reheat Coils**

   a. When hot water reheat coils are selected for location in ductwork running in the ceiling space over occupied areas designed under rigid acoustical criteria, . . .

The **design checklist** used by some offices is quite similar to a specification checklist. It contains some items common to every project using that particular design, and other items infrequently used but of prime importance to some projects. (A sample page showing a portion of a typical design checklist is shown in Exhibit 22.)

The design checklist

Some consulting offices develop **standard details** which show their preferred methods of assembly or arrangement. This makes it unnecessary to redesign them on each project. Usually a standard detail reflects the firm's best method of design to date. Many firms have them reproduced on transparencies which can be attached to the final drawings by adhesive. They reason this saves drafting time and, more important, removes the possibility of drafting

The use of standard details — dangers and benefits

EXHIBIT 22
MECHANICAL — DESIGN CHECKLIST
X Y Z Inc.

3. Outdoor Conditions — Cold Weather Design
Rain and Snow Design — Ventilation Louvers

ITEMS (Continued)	Checked by:
c. Are the outside air intake louvers located above normal snow collection or drift line?	yes - JRP
d. Are the "storm-proof" louver blades specified on outside air intake louvers?	yes - JRP
e. Is a proper drainage method shown on drawing detail to permit moisture carry-over to drain from louver and from any connecting ductwork?	Yes - see dwg. M-17, detail C. - JRP
f. Does the outside air intake louver specified have low enough air velocity at design air quantity to prevent moisture carry-over?	Yes - see catalog data in file. - JRP
g. Are the outside air intake and exhaust air louvers located other than facing into prevailing wind?	yes - Prev. wind from N.W. - louvers on S.W. - JRP
h. Check air friction pressure drop across all louvers at design air quantities and design velocities. (File copy of catalog selection chart of each manufacturer specified and mark design point on chart or curve.)	O.K. = 0.05"WG @ 400 FPM - JRP

errors. The merit in using standard details is questioned by other design professionals. These firms view such use as a lazy way to design, and consider them more trouble than help. This is especially true if 1) they are improperly used and 2) if any error or omission results in tying them to the rest of the design. If you use standard details, apply them **only** when they are appropriate. Never alter your design requirements. Drafting convenience is **always** subservient to design excellence. Properly applied, standard details serve you well; misapplied, this error control method may do more harm than good. A small error or omission in using a standard is usually considered more negligent than a larger error in using a nonstandard item.

There are many opinions on how to check drawings. However, the use of design manuals and design checklists has been singled out by several claims-free firms as being particularly helpful in reducing the chance of error or omission.

Rigid formats can stifle design progress. Some projects are so unusual that an established design procedure may not be practiced. In those instances, your judgment must prevail in selecting the proper design and checking procedures.

Remember, however, that when a **routine** application of a **conventional** system is used, a very small error may be all that is necessary to convince a jury that you were negligent. By contrast, the same error made on a project somewhat experimental in nature with an unconventional system might not be deemed negligence on your part by a court. The professional liability lesson: use procedural checking aids wherever practical. By doing so, you may eliminate many frustrating errors or omissions in routine design activities.

C. Bid Period

Once the project is out to bid, another of the many pressure-laden stages of the construction process comes into being. How you respond to questions put to you by bidding contractors just before bids are due is of major importance to your professional liability well-being.

Few problems arise when there is sufficient time to issue a written addendum and to make sure it reaches all parties concerned. Incredible complications can result if you depart from these prearranged and well-established communication methods. (See Chapter II, Contracts, Discussions, Conferences.)

How do you handle this situation in your own practice?

Contractors, subcontractors and material suppliers who are assembling bid figures may call your office to press for last minute interpretations of your drawings and specifications. In an effort to be cooperative, your employees may be tempted to clarify an apparent ambiguity and discover later there is insufficient time before bid opening to issue the same clarification to all potential bidders. Consequently, one bidder may gain an unfair competitive advantage over the others or an answer given in such a hurry may turn out to be wrong. In either case, you may be exposed to allegations that you and your employees performed negligently.

Outline ahead of time the type of response you wish to give in such circumstances.

One design professional has posted a notice in his drafting room to assist his employees in handling this problem. Copies of the notice are located near each telephone. The content of the notice is similar to that shown in Exhibit 23.

Other design professionals attack the same problem from a different angle, by cautioning the bidding contractors and subcontractors to refrain from using unauthorized data in arriving at their bids. Another design professional calls the attention of the bidders to the importance of the obligation they will undertake by dispatching to all general contractor bidders a carefully drafted letter of explanation similar to Exhibit 24 and an extra copy of the warranty they will be required to execute (Exhibit 25).

EXHIBIT 23

Advising Employees About Communicating During Bid Period
X Y Z Inc.
*(To be posted in **all** departments)*

NOTICE
TO ALL EMPLOYEES

If you receive a telephone call or a personal visit from a contractor, subcontractor or material supplier during the bid period on a project, and he asks for a clarification or interpretation, contending there is an error or ambiguity on the drawings or specifications —

DO NOT VOLUNTEER YOUR OWN OPINION NO MATTER HOW CONVINCED YOU ARE THAT YOU KNOW THE ANSWER!

DO THE FOLLOWING:

1. Tell the caller he most conform with the instructions contained in General Conditions on Instruction to Bidders. If he persists, refer him to your department head.

2. If the department head is not available and the caller insists he must have an immediate answer, then respond as follows:

   a. Carefully write down the content of the caller's request and his assertions as to what and why any portions of the drawings or specifications are ambiguous or in error. **(DO NOT EXPRESS YOUR OPINION AS TO WHETHER HE IS CORRECT OR NOT.)**

   b. Tell him you **cannot** give him the information he desires because it may give him a competitive advantage not enjoyed by others bidding or quoting on the project.

   c. Inform him that you will pass the request to your department head but that any clarification, correction or change in the drawings or specifications must be issued in the form of an addendum or change order as is appropriate.

d. If there appears to be insufficient time to issue an addendum, tell the caller that you cannot advise him verbally, and that he must arrive at his own conclusions based on the content of the drawings and specifications as they are, without any assistance from you, pending issuance of an addendum or a possible extension of the bid period.

EXHIBIT 24

X Y Z, Inc.

General Contractor
Any City, U.S.A.

Re: Very Large Project

Gentlemen:

As the Owner's representative, we are taking this opportunity to point out one especially important provision of the Construction Contract Documents, Instructions to Bidders — the *Bidder's Warranty* (extra copy enclosed).

Your careful reading of the Bidder's Warranty is imperative because by signing and submitting it with your bid figure, you will be assuring the Owner that your detailed examination of the Drawings and Specifications has turned up no ambiguities which need clarification, that only authorized data have been used to arrive at your bid figure, and also that the experience and capabilities of your firm, your workmen and your subcontractors are particularly well-suited to the construction of this type of project.

Please take special note that **each** of your **subcontractors** must also submit a signed copy of the Bidder's Warranty before the Owner can award the contract.

If you find that you are unable to sign this warranty because you believe the Drawings or Specifications are inadequate or erroneous in some way, please notify us at once so that corrective action can be taken. Similarly, if your bid figure is affected by information not contained in the Construction Contract Documents, contact us immediately before submitting your bid.

Very truly yours,

JOHN Q. ENGINEER

EXHIBIT 25

BIDDER'S WARRANTY

By the act of submitting a bid for the proposed contract, the Bidder warrants that:

1. The Bidder and all subcontractors he intends to use have carefully and thoroughly reviewed the Drawings, Specifications and other Construction Contract Documents and have found them complete and free from ambiguities and sufficient for the purpose intended; further that,

2. The Bidder and all workmen, employees and subcontractors he intends to use are skilled and experienced in the type of construction represented by the Construction Contract Documents bid upon; further that,

3. Neither the Bidder nor any of his employees, agents, intended suppliers or subcontractors have relied upon any verbal representations, allegedly authorized or unauthorized from the Owner, his employees or agents including architects, engineers or consultants, in assembling the bid figure; and further that,

4. The bid figure is based solely upon the Construction Contract Documents and properly issued written Addenda and not upon any other written representation.

In an effort to emphasize to the bidders the importance of giving consideration to the effects of site conditions upon construction processes, one design professional adds a requirement to the Bidder's Warranty similar to the following:

The Bidder also warrants that he has carefully examined the site of the Work and that from his own investigations he has satisfied himself as to the nature and location of the Work and the character, quality, quantities of materials and difficulties to be encountered, the kind and extent of equipment and other facilities needed for the performance of the Work, the general and local conditions, and other items which may, in any way, affect the Work or its performance.

Remember that a written warranty that becomes part of the Construction Contract Documents is a legal document. These professional liability loss prevention methods used by others should be reviewed by your attorney before you adopt them to determine whether they are effective in your particular jurisdiction.

D. Shop Drawing Review

1. Complete and Timely Processing

The shop drawing is the connecting link between the design and the construction. It is the designer's method of feeling the contractor's pulse. Because of the increasing complexity of today's construction, the informational conduit known as the shop drawing has in recent years become a most productive source of professional liability claims against the designer. Formerly, when building construction was relatively simple and a supply of skillful workmen was abundant, the shop drawing submittal was of subsidiary importance. Now this is not the case. So many claims against design professionals are directly or indirectly connected with the shop drawing submittal that it ranks in importance equal to the drawings and specifications.

Unreasonable delay in processing and ambiguous wording in the shop drawing stamp are the two most noteworthy sources of trouble. Most specifications require that the contractor refrain from ordering material until he has received the results of a review of his shop drawing submittal from the design professional. Any delay in processing shop drawings affects the contractor's scheduling and, in turn, may result in extra cost to the owner.

Suggested office procedures for reducing the risk of delay are as follows:

a. **Record** in a log book and **date stamp** all incoming shop drawings without regard to the size of the project involved. Immediately stamp each separate binder or group of shop drawings when received with the date, time and the firm name. Record each category of equipment, material, or construction method comprising a shop drawing submittal together with the quantity of copies received. (For an example of a shop drawing log see Exhibit 26.)

EXHIBIT 26

XYZ, Inc.
Shop Drawing Log

Spec Section: MECHANICAL

Project: VERY TALL OFFICE BLDG.   Client: JOHN DOE, ARCHITECT

Location: ILLINOIS CITY   Recorder: RICHARD ROE

Mfr. & Title	Spec. Item	Date Rec'd	No. Copies Rec'd	No. Copies Ret'd	Date Ret'd	Action Taken	Checked By
P & Q PUMPS	M-47	8/6/78	7	6	8/18/79	FURNISH AS SUBMITTED	H.H. LD.

b. Make certain that the office personnel who record and stamp the shop drawings are instructed to deliver the drawings to the proper principal, project manager, or authorized person immediately after recording and stamping.

c. Maintain a tickler file of all shop drawings currently being processed. To be fair to the contractor, designate a maximum number of days or hours permitted to process the shop drawings. Assign the duties of keeping the tickler file to certain office personnel. Have them responsible for the follow-up every day (or some appropriate time interval) until the shop drawings leave the office. If some special problems prevent completion of the review within the designated period, have this brought to the attention of the proper person. He may want to send a letter of explanation to the client or contractor.

Another valuable loss abatement tool in the checklist family of aids is the **shop drawing checklist.** Many routine items are checked in a shop drawing review. Some firms have developed detailed checklists for complex submittals noting each individual point to be investigated and verified. Most of these checklists need to be continually expanded or updated. (See Exhibit 27 for a page from one version of a general shop drawing checklist.)

2. Your Shop Drawing Stamp

Why is the contractor required to submit shop drawings? The submittal serves to demonstrate that the contractor understands the intent of the design. He marks his progress by furnishing information as to what materials, equipment, and methods he plans to use.

To guard against any misinterpretation of your intent, use extreme care in selecting words which describe the type of action you designate in notes on the stamp impression. Words like "approved"

EXHIBIT 27

SHOP DRAWING CHECKLIST
X Y Z, Inc.
MECHANICAL CONSULTING ENGINEERS

Project: VERY TALL OFFICE BUILDING

Client: JOHN DOE, ARCHITECT

Project Location: ILLINOIS CITY

Date: 8/11/79

Submittal Description (Manufacturer, Etc.) P&Q Co. — Heating
Water pumps, primary and secondary

	GENERAL ITEMS	COMMENTS 1st Checker	2nd Checker
1.	Item manufacturer submitted was one specified	yes ✓ H.H.	✓ LD
2.	Item manufacturer submitted, a substitution not specified	no H.H.	✓ LD
3.	Item model/type submitted is that specified	yes ✓ H.H.	✓ LD
4.	Item submitted has performance (capacity) specified	yes ✓ H.H.	✓ LD.
5	Item motor electrical data submitted matches electrical service to motors	yes ✓ H.H.	✓ LD.
6.	Item motor type matches that specified	yes ✓ H.H.	✓ LD.
7.	Item pressure ratings match specified	yes ✓ H.H.	✓ LD.
8.	ASME codes and ratings match specified	NOT REQ'D. H.H.	✓ LD.
9.	Item optional accessories submitted match those specified	yes ✓ H.H.	✓ LD.
10.	Specified certifications of testing submitted	yes ✓ H.H	✓ LD

What do "approved"
and "approval" mean
on shop drawings?

or "approval" should be avoided. Experience has shown that when persons outside the construction industry are called upon to determine what the engineer means when he "approves" a shop drawing, they often take it to imply **unqualified acceptance.** It is advisable to use other words more exactly descriptive of your intent. Some engineering firms have attempted to solve this problem by the use of phrases such as:

a. Furnish as submitted
b. No exceptions taken.

Other wordings often used are

a. Furnish as corrected
b. Submit specified item
c. Rejected
d. Revise and resubmit.

Almost all shop drawing stamps currently in use include the name of the design professional firm and spaces for the date and the name of the person authorized to sign the shop drawing stamp impression on behalf of the firm. Some examples of stamp impressions used are shown in Exhibits 28, 29 and 30.

EXHIBIT 28
SHOP DRAWING STAMPS

**ITEMS SHOWN ON THE SHOP DRAWINGS
MAY BE FURNISHED WITH CORRECTIONS SHOWN
IN ACCORDANCE WITH THE FOLLOWING:**

Corrections or comments made on the shop drawings during this review do not relieve contractor from compliance with requirements of the drawings and specifications. This check is only for review of general conformance with the design concept of the project and general compliance with the information given in the contract documents. The contractor is responsible for: confirming and correlating all quantities and dimensions; selecting fabrication processes and techniques of construction; coordinating his work with that of all other trades; and performing his work in a safe and satisfactory manner.

X Y Z, Inc.

Date _____ **By** _____

**ITEMS SHOWN ON THE SHOP DRAWINGS MAY BE
FURNISHED AS SUBMITTED IN ACCORDANCE WITH
THE FOLLOWING:**

Corrections or comments made on the shop drawings during this review do not relieve contractor from compliance with requirements of the drawings and specifications. This check is only for review of general conformance with the design concept of the project and general compliance with the information given in the contract documents. The contractor is responsible for: confirming and correlating all quantities and dimensions; selecting fabricaton processes and techniques of construction; coordinating his work with that of all other trades; and performing his work in a safe and satisfactory manner.

X Y Z, Inc.

Date _____ **By** _____

EXHIBIT 29
SHOP DRAWING STAMPS

☐ REVIEWED   ☐ REVISE AND RESUBMIT

☐ REJECTED   ☐ FURNISH AS CORRECTED

Corrections or comments made on the shop drawings during this review do not relieve contractor from compliance with requirements of the drawings and specifications. This check is only for review of general conformance with the design concept of the project and general compliance with the information given in the contract documents. The contractor is responsible for: confirming and correlating all quantities and dimensions; selecting fabricaton processes and techniques of construction; coordinating his work with that of all other trades; and performing his work in a safe and satisfactory manner.

X Y Z, Inc.

Date _____ **By** _____

☐NO EXCEPTION TAKEN   ☐ MAKE CORRECTIONS
                                 NOTED

☐REJECTED   ☐ REVISE AND RESUBMIT
         ☐SUBMIT SPECIFIED ITEM

Checking is only for general conformance with the design concept of the project and general compliance with the information given in the contract documents. Any action shown is subject to the requirements of the plans and specifications. Contractor is responsible for: dimensions which shall be confirmed and correlated at the job site; fabrication processes and techniques of construction; coordination of his work with that of all other trades; and the satisfactory performance of his work.

X Y Z, Inc.

Date _____ **By** _____

EXHIBIT 30
SHOP DRAWING STAMPS

ITEMS SHOWN ON THE SHOP DRAWINGS ARE

REJECTED

X Y Z, Inc.

Date _____ By _____

REVISE AND RESUBMIT

SHOP DRAWING REVIEW

REVIEW IS FOR GENERAL COMPLIANCE
WITH CONTRACT DOCUMENTS
NO RESPONSIBILITY IS ASSUMED FOR
CORRECTNESS OF DIMENSIONS OR DETAILS

NO EXCEPTIONS TAKEN	
MAKE CORRECTIONS NOTED	
AMEND & RESUBMIT	
REJECTED — SEE REMARKS	

X Y Z, Inc.

Date _____ **By** _____

As a professional you do not want to evade your responsibilities, but you should define your limits so others can understand and appreciate them. To communicate more exactly with the contractor, define your specific intent and the limits of your review in the "Definitions" section of your specification. Make it clear that when some errors are detected but others are overlooked, this does not grant the contractor permission to proceed in error; that regardless of **any** information

**The limits of
your responsibility**

177

contained in the shop drawings, the requirements of the drawings and specifications must be followed and are not waived or superseded in any way by the shop drawing review. Then put this definition into actual practice; never use the shop drawing review to change the requirements of the contract documents. Use other means of communication such as the Change Order to alter the contractual obligations of the contractor. Nothing you do will gain the respect of the contractor more surely than for you to accurately and consistently distinguish between those items legimately a part of his agreed obligations and those items which were not originally specified. True, other components may become necessary or desirable and, if so, he should be given extra compensation. Be sure your client thoroughly understands your responsibilities during this phase of construction interplay. He should realize that you always intend to act in an equitable fashion with the contractor. Explain the need for a certain amount of leeway **before** the circumstances arise. If you conduct your shop drawing review in this manner and communicate your intentions accurately, the words you use on your shop drawing stamp will be more effective and mean more to the contractor.

Look at your own shop drawing stamp and then ask yourself if it could be improved in any way. Talk with your attorney about it. Do not take the examples shown on Exhibits 28, 29 and 30 as the ultimate word. You may find an even better way to get your shop drawing review message across in an unmistakably clear manner.

E. The Importance of Improving Technical Quality

From some of the statements made herein you may have the impression that all claims against design professionals are caused by matters remote from their specialty. Most are! However, you must never lose sight of a fundamental requisite: a high level of competence in the technical sense is necessary for a good reputation and a clean professional liability record. A repeated source of claims within the technical functions lies in the specification of materials and equipment. The trouble appears to grow from the failure to properly evaluate available information about materials and systems that you specify. Certain designers have admirable mathematical capabilities but fail to reflect this exacting quality in their specification of materials. Others take elaborate care to produce complete and accurate drawings and specifications but ignore recently developed techniques. Frequently these techniques, if incorporated in a design, could reduce the number of problems encountered by the contractor in installation or by the owner in operation.

The technical quality you struggle to attain is not limited to error-free drawings and specifications in the academic sense. It also includes constant vigilance to eliminate things that will tend to add confusion and controversy to a design. As one design professional puts it, "You must constantly strive to remove all possible 'idiot factors' from your drawings and specifications." It follows that you can turn a good design into a problem job by designing controversy into your drawings and specifications. This section is devoted to these troublesome features of your practice.

1. Back to School

Experience is not the same as competency. If one of your design-employees is strong on practical experience but weak in his academic background, he may commit technical errors. This statement is not intended to discount the value of experience: practical knowledge gained from past applications is essential. You can, however, greatly increase your chances of professional survival by continually adding to your store of technical knowledge and to that of your key personnel. By using this approach you can often make very competent designers out of those in your firm who may have limited formal training.

Whatever your particular field, are you sure your firm is not falling behind in knowledge of the advancements being made in your special area?

Practical experience v. academic training

**Updating your
technical know-how:
a matter of survival**

When was the last time you or your key people attended a technical seminar or a university extension course on a related subject? The updating of expertise is not a matter of **success** but of **survival.** This is amply demonstrated in recent professional liability claims where archaic methods were the source of the trouble.

Some design professionals tend to belittle the value of revitalizing their training. It may be that their apathy is based on belief that although great technical advances are being made in the science field, these breakthroughs have only rare application in the construction industry. Attempts to upgrade your technical capabilities can prove fruitful. Bits of information gleaned from technical society journals and ingenious design features created and offered to the profession by other professionals can be extremely helpful in increasing your technical ability.

The assembly of design manuals, discussed previously, may serve as an educational tool. Anyone who writes a design manual must, of necessity, have a very detailed knowledge of the technical aspects of design. By compiling this information for the use of others, the writer of the manual strengthens and broadens his own knowledge of the subject matter. There are also many other valuable dividends from this procedure.

Many firms make it a standard practice to encourage those with inadequate academic backgrounds to attend classes. As an incentive, some firms pay a part or all of any tuition fees charged. The rewards to both the student and the firm more than justify this expenditure. Examine your own policies regarding the technical improvement of your staff. Do not fail to recognize that, in addition to improved performance, you are also decreasing the likelihood of crippling errors or omissions. The level of competence of your staff has a direct relationship to your professional liability future.

2. Untried, Untested, and Undesirable

Imagine yourself confronted with this dilemma — Manufacturer X hopes you will specify his material. His company has just finished a complete redesign of a particular product, giving him a competitive price advantage. The manufacturer advises you to "keep up with the latest technical advances. Do not use outmoded techniques or you will be wasting the client's money."

Now suppose that Manufacturer Y warns you to "beware of new material that is not time-tested. Stick with the product you know and have used with success." This company has not changed their product in several years.

Suppose further that another design professional is the client. The client (an architect) complains that you (a structural engineer) are not progressive or flexible enough, that **you** cannot adapt to modern techniques and this cramps **his** style. He feels his design freedom is hampered by the material you insist should be used.

You investigate Manufacturer X's product and find that the new material is much less rigidly constructed than before, weighs only half as much as the old material and contains components made by other manufacturers whose names are unfamiliar to you. You are naturally suspicious of the predicted performance.

Which product do you choose? Do you specify both or neither? Chances are that this situation is not new to you. As you probably have discovered many times before, this type of decision is not always easy to make. Insofar as this decision relates to your professional liability, keep in mind that you should study with great care any new material or method before specifying its use. A much more prudent path, if you have any doubts, is to wait for a reasonable period before specifying a new product or a newly conceived structural component. If possible, observe the product in operation for a time. Some manufacturers, pressed for profits, have a disconcerting habit of experimenting outside the laboratory, i.e., in the market place, with an unsuspecting owner's money. Do not be a party to this type of business practice.

Designing is not an exact science. Even with the best components at hand, trouble sometimes occurs. However, because they do not fully understand your role, laymen may believe you have complete control over the manufacture of the equipment you specify and may assume that you test each item before specifying its use. What happens when these same laymen, serving as jurors, are presented with a dispute involving a complicated design problem? It is common in such cases for a court to award immense damages in a claim against a designer even though the merit of the claim is questionable in other designers' minds.

In order to protect yourself from this disturbing tendency, you must exploit every means at your disposal to steer clear of litigation. This caution should not, however, stifle your ingenuity. Some of the most applauded design advances have come about by the novel application of tested and proven materials.

**Experiment —
but carefully**

Every single project you design has an element of the experimental in it. Nowhere else at any time has there been built the exact combination of systems you have designed. This experimental side of your profession makes it hazardous enough; do not endanger your reputation by introducing more unknown quantities. Experiment if you must, but experiment in areas where you have a strong probability of success. Before you abandon the specifications of those materials or methods which have given reliable performance in the past, consider carefully how a product failure will affect your professional reputation.

If a client insists, against your better judgment, that you pursue a certain design path, be very wary. If the product is obviously experimental in nature and successful performance is questionable, seek the advice of your attorney or insurance broker.

Somewhere between technical design obsolescence and radical design innovation lies a safer middle ground. You must search for it as though your future depended upon it. It does!

V

insurance

V

insurance

A. How Good is Your Insurance?

It is impossible to quickly cover all aspects of a design professional's insurance. (See Quick Reference Insurance Analyzer, Exhibit 31.) Nevertheless, there are certain aspects of your professional liability insurance which you should understand since they might become very important if a claim is brought against you alleging professional deficiency.

If you are like most people, you find reading insurance policies a bore. Policies seem to be intricate, tricky and composed of extremely fine print. This places them low on your priority of things to be read. Nonetheless, if you wish to reduce your professional liability loss exposure, it is important to know what the policy provisions mean. Additionally, you should know which of your professional activities are not or cannot be insured.

A professional liability insurance policy is like any complex thing; if you pull it apart and study its components, you find that its complexity diminishes. Let us do this

Dissecting the professional liability policy

EXHIBIT 31

QUICK REFERENCE INSURANCE ANALYZER

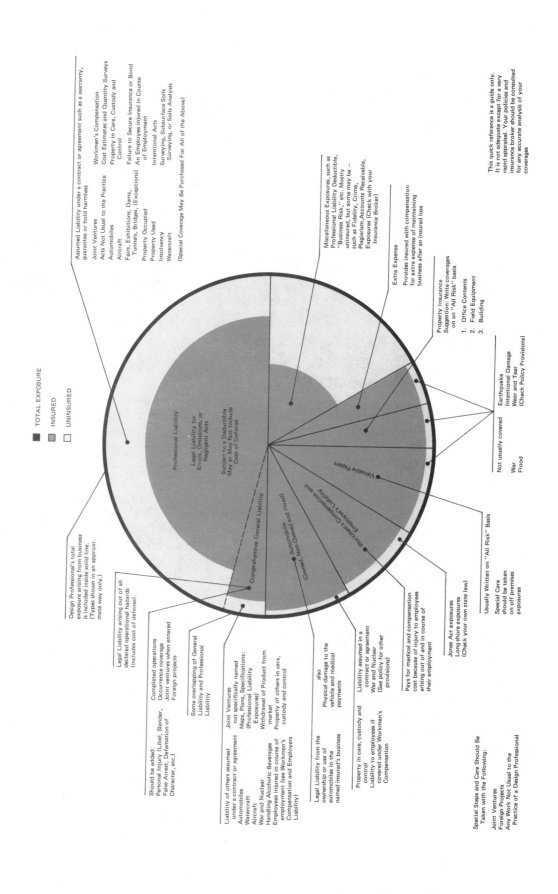

TOTAL EXPOSURE

INSURED

UNINSURED

Design Professional's total exposure arising from business is included inside solid line. (Types shown in an approximate way only.)

Legal Liability arising out of all declared operational hazards (includes cost of defense).

Should be added:
Personal Injury (Libel, Slander, False Arrest, Defamation of Character, etc.)

Completed operations
Occurrence coverage
Joint ventures when entered
Foreign projects

Some overlapping of General Liability and Professional Liability

Liability of others assumed under a contract or agreement
Automobiles
Watercraft
Aircraft
War and Nuclear
Handling Alcoholic Beverages
Employees injured in course of employment (see Workmen's Compensation and Employers Liability)

Joint Ventures not specifically named
Maps, Plans, Specifications: (Professional Liability Exposures)
Withdrawal of Product from market
Property of others in care, custody and control

Legal Liability from the ownership or use of automobiles in the named insured's business

Property in care, custody and control
Liability to employees if covered under Workmen's Compensation

also
Physical damage to the vehicle and medical payments

Liability assumed in a contract or agreement
War and Nuclear
(See policy for other provisions)

Pays for medical and compensation cost because of injury to employees arising out of and in course of their employment

Jones Act exposures
Long shore exposures
(Check your own state law)

Usually Written on "All Risk" Basis

Special Care should be taken on off premises exposures

Special Steps and Care Should Be Taken with the Following:

Joint Ventures
Foreign Projects
Any Work Not Usual to the Practice of a Design Professional

Comprehensive General Liability

Automobile (Owned, Non-Owned and Hired)

Workmen's Compensation and Employer's Liability

Professional Liability

Legal Liability for Errors, Omissions, or Negligent Acts

Subject to a Deductible May or May Not Include Cost of Defense

Valuable Papers

Assumed Liability under a contract or agreement such as a warranty, guarantee or hold harmless
Joint Ventures
Acts Not Usual to the Practice
Automobiles
Aircraft
Fairs, Exhibitions, Dams, Tunnels, Bridges, (Exceptions)
Property Occupied
Property Used
Insolvency
Watercraft
(Special Coverage May Be Purchased For All of the Above)

Workmen's Compensation
Cost Estimates and Quantity Surveys
Property in Care, Custody and Control
Failure to Secure Insurance or Bond
An Employee injured in Course of Employment
Intentional Acts
Surveying, Subsurface Soils
Surveying, or Soils Analysis

Miscellaneous Exposures, such as Professional Liability Deductible, "Business Risk," etc. Mostly uninsured, but some may be — such as Fidelity, Crime, Plagiarism, Accounts Receivable, Exposures (Check with your Insurance Broker)

Extra Expense
Provides insured with compensation for extra expense of maintaining business after an insured loss

Property Insurance
Suggestion: Write coverages on an "All Risk" basis
1. Office Contents
2. Field Equipment
3. Building

Earthquake
Intentional Damage
Wear and Tear
(Check Policy Provisions)

Not usually covered
War
Flood

This quick reference is a guide only. It is not adequate except for a very rapid appraisal. Your policies and insurance broker should be consulted for any accurate analysis of your coverages with a professional liability insurance form so that you can have a quick understanding of what is and what is not usually covered. You can thereby assess your own position relative to the coverage you now have. By doing this, do not conclude that you should ever discount the services of a competent agent or broker. Only a competent insurance man has the experience and judgment necessary to give thorough counsel on the adequacy of your insurance coverage. You may make a cursory evaluation of your insurance program, but you should rely upon professional advice for final judgment. You should also ascertain that the insurance broker with whom you work has a special interest in serving design professionals. Without this special interest, he may not have the expertise necessary to make a proper assessment of your needs and your professional liability insurance problems.

1. Insuring Agreement

Now let us see what makes a professional liability insurance form tick. The first section you should study may be called the "Professional Liability Coverage Agreement." This is often the first paragraph in the policy or section providing professional liability coverage. It sets forth the basis upon which the Company will pay in behalf of you, the Named Insured. Most underwriters say they will pay because of "error, omission or negligent acts" or on account of "an occurrence" (which is defined in the policy). This means that the Company will be responsible to the Named Insured for damages which arise out of his professional performance and which are **unexpected.** Although this terminology is not defined in writing, it is usually reflected in the underwriters' attitude if a claim is presented; that is, they do not feel obligated to pay for an expected result. Nor do they intend to pay for poor business judgment or violation of a confidence or trust.

2. Exclusions

The second most important section of the professional liability form is titled "Exclusions." This section starts out by stating **"This insurance does not apply (to): ."** This curtails the coverage afforded in the

Coverage

189

Insuring Agreement. Typically, a professional liability policy will **not** insure the following:

- Liability assumed under any type of agreement, contract, warranty, guarantee, certificate, whether it be written or oral;

- Liability arising out of the ownership or use of any type of vehicle or conveyance;

- Liability for injury to, or death of, any employee arising out of, and in the course of, his employment;

- Obligation to pay workers' compensation, unemployment compensation, disability benefits, etc.;

- Liability arising out of the ownership, use, or maintenance of property owned by the Named Insured;

- Activities which are not customary or usual to the performance of the particular professional services designated in the form (they do not want to insure a design professional for medical malpractice);

- Liability arising out of some types of cost estimates or quantity surveys;

- Property in the Named Insured's care, custody and control, or rented or leased to the Named Insured;

- Liability attributable to a failure by the Named Insured to effect or maintain an insurance policy or bond;

- Liability arising out of operations in connection with tunnels, bridges, dams (with certain qualifications);

- Loss caused intentionally by, or at the direction of, an Insured;

- Liability arising out of surveying activity, ground

testing, subsurface soils surveying;

- Loss that is the result of the insolvency of the Named Insured.

There may be others. Each form is different and should be read carefully so that you are aware of the extent of the **Exclusions** in your policy. Many of the exclusions may be bought back; that is, you pay an additional premium and have an endorsement added to your professional liability form which will delete the exclusion.

If you would like a closer look at some of the exclusions and the reasons for them, consider the following:

- The exclusion relating to liability assumed by the insured under any contract or agreement including any hold harmless and indemnity clause, warranties, guarantees or penalty clauses is aimed at situations where an insured might expand the liability that he has implicit as a matter of law to special liability that might be the result of his agreement to assume a greater burden of responsibility than is normally expected of a design professional in private practice. Not only should an insured be wary about hold harmless and indemnity clauses, but any type of clause that calls for a special level of performance, a certification of any type, a guarantee, warranty, etc. A design professional is insured against deficiencies in his professional performance when measured against others in his profession in his locale. Any agreement to go beyond that might be construed as falling within the intent of this exclusion and negate the effect of coverage.

- The exclusion relating to the ownership or use of any type of conveyance (i.e. automobile, mobile equipment, aircraft, watercraft, etc.) is obvious. It is not the intent of your professional liability insurance carrier to provide coverage that should be provided by a company qualified to issue that type of coverage.

- Workers' Compensation, Unemployment Compensation, Disability Benefit Coverage, etc. are provided by other insurance forms. The exclusion relating to these exposures underscores that fact.

- The same is true of liability that is the result of injury to one of your employees arising out of and in the course of their employment. This is a Workers' Compensation exposure and should be covered elsewhere.

- Perhaps one of the largest areas of concern to professional liability underwriters in today's climate is any liability that would result in any way from the ownership, maintenance, or use of any property of the insured or in the conduct of any business enterprise (other than that of being a design professional in private practice) which is wholly or partly owned by the insured. The importance of this exclusion(s) and its (their) professional liability implications cannot be overstated. Courts in the United States have held that certain doctrines of liability do not apply to design professionals in private practice so long as they do not have an ownership interest in the "product" that may have caused injury. There are two common doctrines used in the products liability field today, breach of implied warranty and strict liability, that could be used to fix liability against a design professional but only so long as he had an ownership interest in the property involved. It is for this reason that it is extremely important for you, as a professional person, to maintain a strict arm's length attitude with any client or project upon which you are asked to do design work. Any deviation from your role as solely a professional to one of entrepreneur might destroy any protection that you might have against claims based upon breach of implied warranty or strict liability (Allied Properties v. Blume).

- It is obvious that a professional liability insurance underwriter is willing to insure you in connection with your professional services as a design professional in private practice, but does not want to insure activities which they are not able to properly underwrite. This would be anything that is not customary or usual to the performance of design professional services for others. It might include the development of a product, income from patents, running a turkey ranch or selling insurance. It is not the company's intent to provide coverage for activities of that nature.

• Neither is it the company's intent to provide the design professional with coverage for damage to property that is owned, rented, or leased to the insured. This exclusion reinforces the underwriters' attitudes about a building for which you have done design and have an ownership interest. This **may** be covered in the general liability portion of the coverage but only if a special endorsement is added to the policy form.

Close attention should be given to the exclusions since the foregoing examination does not begin to exhaust the ramifications that this portion of a professional liability insurance policy might have upon the effectiveness of your insurance.

3. Policy Period and Territory

A third section in an insurance policy is that which determines the **policy period** and **territory.** This part determines the effective time of the insurance policy. It also determines in what geographical areas the policy will be effective. With professional liability coverage the **policy period** (term) looms very important since the particular professional activity that may have **caused** the loss may be quite remote from the **discovery time** or the **occurrence** that gives rise to the loss. This fact may create a labyrinthian exercise for you to arrive at the date upon which coverage is effective. As a rule of thumb, most professional liability insurance forms for design professionals provide coverage on a retroactive basis; that is, they protect against professional activities which may have given rise to a claim and which were performed prior to the policy period, so long as claim is made during the policy period and so long as there

Time and place of coverage

was no knowledge of the occurrence (error or omission) at the effective date of the coverage (and there is no other collectible insurance). They also cover errors, omissions, or negligent acts committed during the policy period if the claim is made during the policy period. This makes it important that you do not change underwriters if you have knowledge of any occurrence (error or omission, etc.) which could be the basis for a claim. In the absence of special provisions which cover you after you retire, it is not normal for coverage to extend beyond the policy period. When a new company, such as a joint venture, is formed for the limited purpose of engaging in a special project, the new business entity requires special treatment from a professional liability insurance point of view. One problem that is created is that, after the project ends, the business entity dissolved, and the insurance coverage discontinued, an alleged error might be discovered. Others exist.

Territory refers to the effective locale of the coverage. Some policies protect you regardless of where the professional liability arises so long as claim is made or suit is brought in the United States or Canada. Others strictly limit coverage to the United States or Canada. If you engage in foreign work you should take special precautions to make certain that your professional liability coverage is broad enough to protect you. Some design professionals feel that it is adequate if coverage protects them only if a claim is made or suit is brought in the United States, but insurance brokers have reason to believe this is not true. There are certain foreign countries whose laws could place you in an embarrassing position, to say the least, if you do not have adequate coverage for the work you perform in their countries. You should carefully check with your insurance broker and the consular or embassy office of the foreign country prior to undertaking the work. In some countries, if anything happens, officials will put you in jail and then proceed to sort out the mess. Other countries' laws read similarly but have rarely been enforced; however, you do not want to be the exception that proves the rule. Then, too, having coverage in some countries that is not written by a company licensed in that country is a violation of law!

4. Settlement

The last section with which you should be especially acquainted will be titled **Settlement.** This portion says that the Company shall not settle any claim without the written consent of the Insured, but that if the Insured should refuse to consent to any settlement recommended, then the Company's liability shall not exceed the amount for which settlement could have been made. Many design professionals feel that this gives the Company a gun which can be used for the purpose of forcing settlement. Fortunately, this is not usually the case. It is true that there may be varying opinions as to whether settlement should or should not be made in a given case, but by and large the underwriters that are providing professional liability insurance for design professionals do not want to make settlement as a pure expedient. This does not mean that they will not consider the potential cost of defense in making an assessment as to the wisdom of settling. They do. However, cost is not their only concern, and a request for settlement when there has been **no** error, omission or negligence may be even more repugnant to them than to you. If you are called upon by your underwriter to agree to a settlement and you do not wish to do so, make certain that the claims manager has a clear understanding of your reasons. If they are logical, he will usually respect them. For your own part, be positive that you are not being unreasonable in the face of a settlement offer by resisting purely on principle. Remember that insurance underwriters are not in the "principle" business. It may be difficult for you, as a design professional, to understand their ambiguous role in this regard. They have to face a cold reality and its economic effect upon themselves and you. Keep in mind that their settlement desire in opposition to your wishes is born of vast experience with many claims.

What about the situation where you are anxious to settle and the Company resists? This does occur. Once a design professional has a taste of a professional liability claim, he may become distraught by the amount of time that the litigation requires. He realizes that the total amount of the claim will not be worth his expenditure in time for defense. He may thus request that the Company accept or arrange settlement. Is this correct? Here again, it is a situation that should be explained clearly and explicitly to the claims manager, with all factors considered. Insurance underwriters normally do not prefer to make gratuitous payments if they feel that your case is well-founded. On the other hand they will not be unreasonable. This is a decision which should be made mutually by you and your underwriter.

B. Getting the Best

Help your underwriter help you

Frequently what **you** do will determine whether you get the best out of your professional liability underwriter or whether you get something less. Since it is quite important in professional liability claims situations that you get the best, some hints on what you can do are in order. Consider the following:

1. Early Claims Reporting

Report claims and potential claims

Your professional liability underwriter would far prefer to have you over-report than under-report claims. It is better to report a dispute situation before it becomes an actual claim than to wait until it is a very hot issue and sides have been drawn up. The claims department of a professional liability insurance company can usually counsel you with methods by which you can reduce your exposure or at least keep things fair. In addition, the claims department can advise you on methods for mitigating damages (if any) so that if you are finally held responsible, the financial burden will be less. By spotting a dispute before it becomes a claim and reporting it to the Company, you may avoid a monumental amount of later grief.

2. The Benefit of Your Input

In the event you are dissatisfied with the progress or defense proceedings that are rendered in your behalf, the claims manager needs the benefit of your thoughts. This does not mean that you should challenge each and every act which you feel is questionable. In fact, this can work to your detriment. Insurance people are human; if you make an exaggerated case out of every small item, you may exhaust your insurance underwriter's patience and great patience may be called for on a later date. On the other hand, claims people recognize that you may have some insight into defense matters which are being missed. Therefore, they welcome any suggestions that you may have to make. They also welcome remarks you may have concerning the adequacy of your defense counsel. In this regard, professional liability underwriters believe a defense attorney must know the subject matter of a professional liability claim thoroughly before he can do his job. Usually he must have had significant experience in the field in order to give you the proper defense. Just as important is the rapport with the person he must defend, you. The Company cannot always tell what the depth of his experience is before they hire him. Your assessment of his capability and his interest in **you** will be a great help to your underwriter's claims manager; not only in respect to any claim you might have, but also for claims in the future.

Communicate with your underwriter

3. Cooperation

It comes as a great shock to most design professionals when they find out how much time and effort they have to put forth to defend themselves against professional liability claims. Your insurance coverage requires that you **cooperate** with the Company, assist in making settlements, attend hearings, trials, etc. This takes valuable time. Nothing is quite so important from the underwriter's point of view than that you show a proper attitude in rendering your aid. This means that any hindrance on your part, perhaps because a small dollar amount is involved, or any hesitancy to attend trials, or aid in gathering witnesses might be interpreted by your underwriter as a lack of cooperation. This can be very damaging to your future underwriting acceptability. Your underwriting reputation can be preserved if you are fully cooperative, do not ask the Company to make policy payments (good-will payments in order to dampen the ire of a client), or otherwise attempt to use your insurance as a mere convenience. Some professional liability underwriters feel that the frequency of using insurance as a business crutch has been far too high. Sooner or later, instances of abuse come to light and when they do, a devastating effect upon the insured's acceptability ensues. A mechanical engineer recently overheard another design professional advise his client: "Well, bring a claim against me. It can't hurt. I've got insurance. I will admit that I did what I thought you wanted. The fact that it didn't turn out may be basis for a claim." That type of reasoning and its effect upon a professional liability underwriter can be ruinous. This attitude comes up with more than sporadic frequency in discussions about professional liability insurance and it should be strictly guarded against. To get the best out of your professional liability insurance, make certain that no accusation can be made that you sought to exploit it.

4. Underwriting Information

To do an adequate design job you need to know all the facts related to your particular piece of work. The same is true of professional liability underwriting. If only some of the facts are available, an inadequate job will be done. Make certain that your professional liability underwriter has all the details which might be germane to your particular operation. This may call for you to put forth a little more effort than is expected of you, but any help you do give will result in better coverage. Too frequently, special types of work are undertaken by design professionals and not made known to the underwriter. When a claim arises and there is an exclusion affecting these infrequent jobs, it can be catastrophic.

Professional liability insurance is a two-way street. If you do your part in connection with its terms and conditions, it can do a better job for you. Make certain that you report claims situations promptly and thoroughly. Also keep in mind that the claims manager needs your help if he is to render the best possible defense. Cooperation should be a key word in all professional liability insurance matters.

C. Builders' Risk "All-Risk" Insurance Protection

A very common type of insurance available to contractors or owners is called Builders' Risk Insurance (or C.O.C., i.e. Course of Construction). Its purpose is to protect the contractor and others having an insurable interest from losses due to disasters such as earthquake, fire, wind, flood, or collapse during the course of construction. The coverage that this insurance affords can protect the design professional from loss of his work product and incidentally from some types of professional liability claims.

The design professional who expends time and money performing construction review of portions of the contractor's work can easily suffer a considerable loss if, due to some act of God, the work is destroyed and must be redone. This insurable interest of the designer is one which can be included within the coverage of a Builders' Risk policy purchased on an "All-Risk" basis. The "All-Risk" type of policy gives extremely broad protection. The prime design professional on the project should routinely include a provision in the General Conditions of the specification requiring the contractor to purchase "All-Risk" Builders' Risk coverage with a sufficient limit to protect the actual replacement value of the work being performed by the contractor.

There are a few other benefits that a design professional may accrue from this type of coverage. If some catastrophe of a type covered by the policy results in a large loss, it is not unusual for the underwriter to seek subrogation against parties involved in the performance of the work in an attempt to recover some of the loss. The underwriter may allege that the designer contributed to the loss by some negligence in performing design services. For example, if a foun-

The design professional should be included in an "All-Risk" policy

dation wall is washed away in a flood, the designer might anticipate an allegation that the wall was negligently designed. Protection against this type of claim can be obtained by seeing to it that the owner or the contractor purchase "All-Risk" Builders' Risk coverage naming the design professional (and others having an insurable interest) as additional insureds. Extending coverage to the design professional will not usually result in any additional cost for the coverage.

By this relatively simple procedure, a possible claims source can be treated very effectively. Detailed questions pertaining to this type of insurance should be directed to your insurance broker.

D. Construction Injuries and Your Liability

Representative of the confusion that exists in design professional liability cases today is a claim involving the death of two men and the injuring of a third by the collapse of a temporary form work erected by a contractor. The plaintiffs contended, and the lower court found, that the design professional firm had been negligent in supervising the work and, in this capacity, failed to act to prevent the collapse of the forms. Ludicrous as this may seem, it does demonstrate the wide gulf in understanding that exists between the design professional and the general public. Fortunately, an Appellate Division looked at the facts with a lucid eye and came up with a conclusion contrary to the findings of the Trial Court.

Construction injuries and the attempt to make them your problem

Similar claims are occurring repeatedly throughout the country. The usual contention is that, because of a design failure or failure in construction review (supervision and inspection) by a design professional, a worker has been injured. The frequency of these claims and the cost of defending them is having a devasting effect upon the professional liability insurability of all design professionals. Such claims are a direct circumvention of the intent of the Workers' Compensation Laws, which were established to give the injured worker prompt and fair recompense for his job-connected injury and his employer immunity from such injury **regardless of**

fault. At the time the laws were first passed, most employers occupied the premises to the exclusion of others while performing their work. This was true in construction as elsewhere. A single general contractor usually performed all phases of construction. With the evolution of specialized trades, there are many parties to the performance of the work on a job site and a climate has been created that allows the contention that some other party has contributed to the injured worker's loss. The fact that his employer is protected by the Workers' Compensation Law while others are not sets up an economic motivation for the injured worker to seek a large amount of recovery from the unprotected parties. You, the design professional, are standing in this highly vulnerable climate every time you perform your professional duties. These types of claims continue to grow in frequency and amount ($1,000,000 being a popular asking price). There have been many rulings against design professionals, some counter to the conclusion drawn by the Appellate Court previously mentioned. If this is the case in your state, what can you do to protect yourself?

On a long-run basis, legislation should be passed which will protect any employer that occupies a common premises with another employer (for a mutual purpose) against claims from injured employees that arise out of, and in the course of, their employment. That was the legislative intent of the original Workers' Compensation Law and it should be re-established so that more than one employer occupying the same premises does not defeat the purpose. Since such legislation may be slow in coming, other defensive methods must be found.

One design professional who has been brushed by the threat of suits from injured employees has established a commendable standard operating procedure. Any job for which he prepares the design and specifications must have, as a condition precedent to his performing the work, a hold harmless and indemnity clause in the General Conditions running from the general contractor to himself and the owner.

The clause which this design professional insists be

inserted in the General Conditions runs as follows:

> The Contractor hereby agrees to hold harmless, indemnify and defend the Owner and his agents, architects, engineers, and employees while acting within the scope of their duties from and against any and all liability, claims, damages and cost of defense arising out of the Contractor's performance of the work described herein but not including the sole negligence of the Owner, his agents, architect and engineers, or employees. The Contractor will require any and all subcontractors to conform with the provisions of this clause prior to commencing any work and agrees to insure this clause in conformity with Paragraph X, Insurance, hereinafter.

A hold harmless clause which HELPS the engineer

This form of hold harmless and indemnity agreement clearly defines the intended status of the parties. The contractor is to be responsible for the injury of his employees or any subcontractor's employees except if the injury is caused by the sole negligence of the owner or design professional. This is a clause for which the contractor can purchase insurance on a reasonable basis, and it tends to protect the design professional from the legal fiction that he is somehow in control of job safety measures. Since the design professional never intends to assume this burden, and since the contractor is usually considered responsible for housekeeping, safety of equipment, scaffolding, and other aspects of the job, the clause seems to be eminently fair.

What alternative steps can you take if you cannot negotiate a similar hold harmless and indemnity clause? You can be protected against the injured employee hazard by using two other methods:

Protecting yourself against the injured worker

1. Make sure that your contract of hire clearly sets out your responsibilities relating to construction review (supervision) and, more importantly, those things for which your are **not** responsible. Typically speaking, you should make certain that a clause with wording similar to the following is in your contract with your client:

> The Design Professional, will make visits to

the job site to observe the progress of the work and to observe whether or not it is, in general, being performed in accordance with his plans and specifications. This does not in any way mean that the Design Professional is a guarantor of the Contractor's work; responsible for safety in, on or about the job site; in control of the safety or adequacy of any equipment, building component, scaffolding, forms, or other work aids; or superintending the work.

(See your attorney to make certain that any clause you adopt is conceived in the right legal connotation for your particular state.)

2. Do as some firms do, include a note on each drawing which states that these drawings do **not** include necessary components for construction safety.

3. Pass legislation similar to that adopted in California, i.e. :

The phrase "supervision of the construction of engineering structures" means the periodic observation of materials and completed work to observe their general compliance with plans, specifications, and design and planning concepts, and does not include responsibility for the superintendence of construction processes, site conditions, operations, equipment, personnel, or the maintenance of a safe place to work or any safety in, on, or about the site of work.

Since the problem of injured workers is looming so large, other devices must be developed. One design professional sends a letter to every contractor that performs work upon his design, pointing out that the contractor is responsible for job safety. He asks that this letter be posted in a prominent place on the job site. Another design professional includes a special clause in the General Conditions which requires that the contractor's Workers' Compensation underwriter have a safety engineer visit the job periodically (only on large jobs) and supply the owner with written reports as to the adequacy of safety measures. These methods can be welded into an imposing chain of protective measures which you can use to reduce or mitigate claims of this nature. Until society recognizes that these types of job-connected injuries are not your responsibility, you must use unrelenting defensive action if you are to avoid their devastating effects.

E. Construction Review

The average design professional who undertakes a project usually agrees to make a reasonable number of visits to the job site to look at the construction and see if the contractor is installing the work as it was designed. The design professional may find defects. If he does, it is his duty to notify the contractor or owner, depending on the contract, so that the error may be corrected. Under no circumstances is it ever the intent to become a guarantor of the contractor's performance by these activities. The fact that a contractor's error goes undetected during the design professional's visit to the site does **not** automatically make the designer negligent; the contractor is never relieved of the responsibility for the discovery of his own errors and the correction of them, nor of the responsibility of properly performing the work.

The contractor is responsible for his own errors

The service that the design professional performs at the construction site has created many controversies and considerable litigation. The reason is the misinterpretation of the scope and intent of the design professional's actions, while he is at the site or while he should be, in someone's opinion, at the site. Many professional liability claims arise out of allegations of negligent construction review. An examination of many of these claims shows that the complainant does not understand the purpose of the field visits. The claims are directed at the design professional even though the problem may arise from faulty installation or defective material. Some complaints allege that even though the contractor's installation was improper, the designer had **inspected** the work, found nothing wrong, and that this, in effect, made the designer partly responsible for the damage. These lawsuits have succeeded in costing the design professional immeasurable time and money, even if there was no actual settlement.

Admittedly, every case must stand on its own facts. Some claims may be justified. The most aggravating problem arises when the design professional's field visit is misunderstood and allegations of negligence are unfair.

It is especially important that you properly communicate and accurately describe what you intend to do when you go to a construction site. The use of words such as "supervision" and "inspection" without accompanying definitions, or the misuse of those same words, may communicate an unintended meaning to jurors. To laymen the word "supervision" without further explanation may carry the connotation that you give direct orders to the contractor's workmen about methods to be used to accomplish a specified objective. If someone is injured during the course of construction and records show that you provided supervision, it is natural for a jury to assume that you are partly to blame.

"Supervision," "inspection," and "construction review"

Attempts to explain to jurors what you really mean by "supervision" may be disregarded. The natural reaction is "if you did not mean supervision, why did you use the word?" Whether you choose to term your field visits "supervision" or "construction review" you should keep one goal firmly in mind: say what you mean in a way likely to be understood by those with little knowledge of what you do.

If you sweep aside those claims which have no merit and examine the ones remaining, one conclusion is clear — inadequate construction review is a major contributing factor to the engineer's present professional liability predicament. Attempts to dispose of the problem by refusing to perform construction review have not been successful. When this tactic has been used, the number of defective installations has increased. Owners and contractors, unable to ascertain the reason for an unsatisfactory result, may claim it was due to design error; thus the burden of defending against unmeritorious allegations is increased enormously. Rather than abdicate your duties, you should attempt to provide higher quality and more frequent construction review. If you divest yourself of this traditional role, you may find you have succeeded in **reducing** your public image to that of a mere technician and in **increasing** your courtroom visits. When seeking to delineate your responsibilities, you must at the same time avoid the impression that you wish to evade your proper responsibilities.

Before you condemn as absurd these exercises in semantics, consider this: until a settled legal definition and outline of the scope of your duties at a construction site are generally recognized and thoroughly understood by the courts, you must use extreme care in the use of words referring to your duties. This is another area where the advice of your attorney may prove quite valuable.

A few firms which make sporadic site visits have made a practice of using the word "observation" in lieu of "inspection." By doing so they hope to avoid the inference that they make continuous and detailed on-site examinations of every facet of the contractor's work. One engineer reflects this practice into punch lists or lists of deficiencies he compiles for the contractor after making visits to the construction site. He labels such lists "Project Observation Reports." (See Exhibit 32.)

F. Choosing An Attorney

If you were to make a visit to any one of the Big Ten campuses during the fall of the year you might discover some boisterous high jinks taking place between the design professional students and the fledgling lawyers. Various forms of competition are concocted which have been scientifically conceived to determine intra-specie superiority. Who can best climb a greased pole, grow a beard, or catch a squealing pig, typify the trials by which superiority is measured. This extracurricular merriment encourages the students to look upon each other as the enemy. Whether the attitude developed during aca-

EXHIBIT 32

PROJECT OBSERVATION REPORT
X Y Z, Inc.

Project: Very Tall Office Bldg.   Client: John Doe

Location: Illinois City   Date: 12/6/79

Reported By: Richard Roe   Copies To: John Doe

of XYZ   James Owner

1. Sections of insulation on the domestic hot water piping have been damaged and must be replaced. Specific locations include 10th, 11th and 16th floors near Column B-14. Request contractor to have __all__ insulation checked for damages before piping is enclosed.

2. Pipe hangers supporting heating water piping on the 14th floor are not equipped with metal shields between the insulation and the hangers. Shields must be added to prevent insulation damage.
(See specification paragraph M-62, page 104.)

demic life is carried over into later practice is moot. One thing is certain: design professionals in private practice make too little use of the former enemy's talent in the conduct of their business. This is unfortunate since he has proficiencies that could save the design professional from needless trouble. The value of an attorney can best be appreciated before trouble arises. His talents and experience are more efficiently used if he is retained in a preventive rather than a defensive way.

How should you go about picking an attorney? First, you must assess your own needs. The legal expert you may require for contract documents, negotiation of fee and other services, may not be the one you will want in the trial court. In choosing legal counsel, you should not base your selection upon social considerations. It is fine to have a lawyer as a friend, but, as in choosing any professional, his qualifications should be placed far ahead of friendship. If you are not experienced in making an assessment of an attorney, consider the following methods used by some design professionals.

1. Referral

   Conversation with your fellow design professionals may bring to light those lawyers who are especially competent in dealing with problems peculiar to your practice. Talk with your colleagues; ask them if they know attorneys familiar with your problems. Seek several opinions in this regard and weigh carefully what you hear.

2. Type of Work

   Most attorneys will not admit to being specialists. The fact remains that certain of them are much more qualified in one field than in another. As a consequence, if you are able to find an attorney who has been heavily involved in construction law or in performance bond defense work, you may have found a man who will be much easier to communicate with and who will understand your problems better than one who has been concentrating on admiralty law. A telephone call to a surety company might elicit the name of a good attorney in the construction field. Contractors are good sources of information about attorneys, particularly those contractors who are connected with your discipline. Of course, you must be careful that no conflict of interest arises out of such a source of information; that is, make sure that the attorney whose services you seek does not also represent a possible adversary. At least a working knowledge of the construction business, terminology, duties and responsibilities are a prerequisite for any attorney who is to successfully look after your interests.

3. Publicity

Professional liability claims affecting design professionals frequently receive wide publicity. Sometimes news articles relate instances where another design professional has been successfully defended in a difficult situation. The next time you read such an item, take the trouble to find out the name of the attorney who represented him. Success in a climate of adversity is a good measure of an attorney's capability. It is interesting how many times you will find the same lawyer's name appearing in connection with suits where defendant design professionals are victorious. Learn who they are. One day you may be in desperate need of such a person.

4. General

There are numerous other considerations in hiring an attorney. Briefly, some are:

a. Ask how much he charges. Attorneys are not reluctant to let you know the basis of their fees and you need not be shy in asking.

b. Seek the names of several design professionals for whom he has performed work. Then ask him if he would object if you contacted them. If he has no objections, do so. The attorney will respect you for your thoroughness. You may learn things that will influence your judgment as to his competence.

c. Ask if he charges for his time when he is

called upon to travel. This could be exceptionally important if he must go to a remote job site or travel to another city in your behalf.

Once you have selected an attorney, be cooperative and loyal. You will find that he does not know everything. You may have to educate him about your problems, but remember when you do, it is for your own good. Keep in mind that today most good attorneys are overwhelmed with work. He may not react with the speed that you expect. Do not give up on him because of this; a delay may be beyond his control. Take him into your confidence and keep him abreast of what you wish to accomplish. His viewpoint may be of great help. Remember that care taken to prevent litigation is much less expensive than defense costs when litigation occurs. Your lawyer knows this. Help him to help you.

G. Glossary

As a businessman, a design professional will be better equipped if he understands the specialized terminology his attorney, insurance broker, and others may use in connection with professional liability claims and insurance. By studying the following pages, the words' meanings may become part of your understanding.

This glossary is in no way intended to contain all possible words; only those that may be obscure to the practicing design professional. It is recommended that you also secure a copy of the "Glossary of Construction Industry Terms" prepared by the American Institute of Architects, 1970. This document will make a fine adjunct to the following pages.

A

A.A.A.: Abbreviation for the American Arbitration Association. (See Arbitration.)

Acceptance: In contract, a demonstration that the offeree is willing to enter into an agreement. (See Contract.)

Accident: In insurance, an unexpected, unusual, unintentional happening that results in damages; usually sudden. (See Occurence.)

Act of God (Insurance): An occurrence, such as flood, earthquake, tornado, caused by the forces of Nature without human intervention, which could not have been averted by reasonable care.

Actual Cash Value (Insurance): The cost of replacing property that is destroyed or damaged at the time of a loss, less accrued depreciation.

Adjuster (Insurance): The insurance underwriter's representative who has authority to settle claims with an insured or third party claimants.

Admissions: A statement by someone relevant to the cause of his adversary. Admissions may be expressed or implied. Their importance to the design professional rests in the fact that they may be damaging in the defense of professional liability claims.

Agency: A contractual relationship, either expressed or implied, whereby one party (the principal) delegates the performance of a task to another (the agent) usually for a consideration. In its broadest sense it includes almost any relationship in which one person acts on behalf of another.

Agent: A person who performs a task or manages an affair for another under an agreement, either expressed or implied, and renders an account to the person for whom he has performed. A prime design professional usually acts as the agent for his client (the owner); a consulting engineer working for an architect acts as his agent. In his relationship with his principal, an agent's first duty is that of good faith and loyalty. Of course, he must not perform in a negligent manner. If he does and his principal suffers damages, he must indemnify him for those damages.

Aggregate Limit: In insurance, the total amount of indemnity payable under a policy of insurance regardless of the number of claims. Typically speaking, the policy will provide a bodily injury limit of $100,000± per person and $300,000± aggregate. The $300,000 limit is the most the company will pay on behalf of the insured during the policy period for bodily injury claims. Professional liability insurance is normally written for architects and engineers with a single limit which is the aggregate; i.e., the face amount of the policy is the maximum per claim and maximum per policy period that will be paid in behalf of the named insured.

Alien Underwriter: An underwriter domiciled in a foreign country.

Allegation: The averment, statement or declaration of a party made in a pleading stating what he expects to prove. In professional liability claims against design professionals, there are usually allegations of errors, omissions, or negligence as a basis for the claim.

All Risk Insurance: Property insurance that provides coverage for all perils except those specifically excluded in the policy form.

Approval (by design professional): Generically, this means that the design professional acquiesces to a particular shop drawing method, material or procedure, but not on an unqualified basis. The design professional's intent is to grant acquiescence only so long as the subject matter is in conformity with the design concept. This has created confusion and misinterpretation. Many design professionals prefer to supplant the term "approval" or "approved" with less ambiguous terminology.

Arbitration: A formalized procedure used for settling disputes between parties to a contract. Makes use of a single arbitrator or a board of arbitrators who listen to the facts without adherence to the rules of evidence recognized in a court of law. Their findings are reduced to writing and become binding upon the parties who have agreed to arbitration contractually. Contracts embodying an arbitration clause frequently make it the sole and exclusive remedy. This creates problems for the design professional because, while arbitration may be a good method for resolving contract disputes, it is not always the best method for handling claims of tort liability. While a dispute may commence out of contract, a counterclaim or allegation may be based upon professional negligence (a tort). The disputants will then find themselves using arbitration to resolve allegations of tort liability, a situation that arbitration is not fully equipped to handle.

Assumption of Risk: An agreement or contract, either expressed or implied, wherein one party assumes the risk connected with the performance or discharge of a duty under the contract or agreement.

Award: The decision rendered by arbitrators in an arbitration proceeding. (See Arbitration.)

B

Backfill: The act in construction of refilling an excavation with earth. Backfill procedures, adequacy and type of material constitute a source of claims against design professionals.

Binder (Insurance): A temporary insurance contract pending issuance of the policy contract. The terms of the binder are implied to be the same as those of the contract to be issued.

Broker (Insurance): A representative of the insured who

purchases insurance from an underwriter and is paid a commission for his services. Some jurisdictions hold that the broker is the agent of the underwriter for collection of premiums.

C

Cancel: In insurance, to interrupt an insurance policy in midterm; to revoke or recall an insurance policy prior to its normal expiration date.

Cause of Action: Basis for bringing suit. The establishment of substantive legal reasons for liability. Importance to design professionals is in the fact that allegations may be made concerning their deportment in their professional performance which does not establish a cause of action. Nonsuit is the result. In some jurisdictions, allegations not sufficient to create a cause of action are answered with a demurrer; i.e., an admission that what is alleged may be true, but is not of sufficient legal consequences to require an answer or further proceedings.

Caveat Emptor: Let the buyer beware. A maxim used in early English mercantile trade that required the purchaser of an article to discover any shortcoming for himself. The risk connected with the sales transaction was placed upon the buyer. (See Caveat Venditor.)

Caveat Venditor: The antithesis of the concept of Caveat Emptor. A maxim placing the responsibility for defects upon the seller, manufacturer, purveyor or perhaps the designer of goods. This maxim is finding support in modern day consumer attitudes. The doctrine of strict liability, i.e., liability without fault for a defect in a manufactured product finds its basis in this maxim. (See Strict Liability.)

Certificate of Insurance: A written statement that a specified insurance is in effect for an insured.

Comprehensive General Liability Insurance: Insurance affording coverage for many types of public liability exposures. This insurance is usually limited to the operational activities of an insured business. However, some underwriters have added the professional coverage to the policy by endorsement. Coverage is designed to insure exposures connected with premises, operations, elevators (if any), independent contractors, completed operations (or products), and automobile exposures. Like all insurance policies, this insurance is afforded subject to the terms, conditions, and exclusions of the contract. Rating may be based upon area, payroll, or gross receipts.

Comprehensive Insurance: Insurance that covers many exposures within a single policy form; usually coverage is provided for all exposures except those specifically excluded. (See Comprehensive General Liability Insurance.)

Construction Review: The on-site duties performed by the design professional to ascertain that the construction is proceeding, in general, with the intent of the plans and specifications. The duties of the design professional performing construction review are limited to the exercise of his professional skill. He is in no way responsible for the operational activities of the contractor, the subcontractor, material men, or other parties on the job site. Construction review is an important aspect of all design professionals' practice since it maintains the integrity of the design concept that supports the qualitative results of the completed work.

Counterclaim: An act in civil procedure whereby the defendant makes claim against the plaintiff on account of a cause of action arising out of the contract that existed at the time of the commencement of action by the plaintiff. Counterclaims are frequently used against design professionals by clients who are seeking to avoid paying their fee. When action is commenced by the design professional, a counterclaim is made by the client alleging professional negligence. This constitutes one of the most frequent of professional liability claims.

D

Damages: The loss, injury, diminution in value caused by negligence, error or omission. Damages are measured at the time of discovery of negligence, error or omission and not at their eventual limit. Thus, if an error is discovered in design prior to construction, the damages are equal to the cost of redesign and not the eventual difference of cost of construction which might be occasioned by correcting the error. (See Robb v. Urdahl, 78 Atlantic 2nd, 386 — 1951.) Damages may be either compensatory or exemplary. Exemplary damages are paid in addition to compensation because of aggravated misconduct on the part of the wrongdoer; they are assessed in order to make an example of him; also called "punitive" damages. There have been rare cases where exemplary damages have been allowed against design professionals; these have not been the result of negligence, but breach of trust. Nonetheless, many summonses and complaints make a prayer for punitive or exemplary damages against design professionals. It can only be assumed that they are asked for in order to increase settlement bargaining power.

Damages, Punitive: Damages assessed to punish; not usually permitted in cases of professional negligence.

Declaratory Relief Action: In insurance when two underwriters have provided coverage for the same insured and there is a question as to which covered the insured for a particular loss, action is brought seeking a declaration from the court, binding on the parties, stating whose coverage shall be in effect. No consideration is given to the subject matter of any claim. This type of action is commonly engaged in when question of coverage exists between two different professional liability underwriters.

Defense: The answer attitude taken by a defendant to a plaintiff's action. This may be legal, procedural, or in the broader sense, behavioral. Any procedure by which an allegation of professional negligence is repelled may be considered the defense. Defense may embody all activity employed by design professionals against claims.

Defect (in design): Some conditions which if implemented by construction would render the facility, building, complex or system unfit for its intended use. A weakness in construction that renders the building unfit or unsafe; some condition rendering construction innately unsafe.

Delegate (Professional Practice): The appointment of another party or person to perform a specific duty. In professional practice certain duties, because they are based on trust and confidence in the professional who assumed the performance of those duties, may not be delegated. (See Scott v. Potomac Insurance Company, 341 Civic 2nd, 1083 — 1959.)

Delivery (of plans and specifications): The transfer, or placing in the possession of a client, plans and specifications in their final and **usable** form. Some jurisdictions hold that delivery is not accomplished until all conditional qualities are removed; i.e., they must be final and complete before delivery is accomplished.

Demand: The same as a claim. The assertion of one's right or due. Design professionals frequently do not recognize a "demand" as being a claim. Any demand for redress on account of alleged error, omission or professional negligence should be reported to your professional liability underwriter just as a "claim" would be reported.

Deposition: The taking of a witness's testimony by interrogation outside the court. The adverse party is given an opportunity to cross-examine.

Derivative Liability: Liability coming from another; liability that was not originated by the primary party. Frequently thought of in connection with joint venture claims. A design professional may enter into a joint venture and become liable because of error, omission or negligence on the part of his co-venturee. This liability is referred to as being derivative, since it is the result of another party's negligence.

Design: Plan of a building, system, equipment, facility, or scheme to be constructed. The schematic portions of plans and specifications used for the purpose of setting forth a building concept. (See Specifications.) In most jurisdictions a design and the specifications are considered a single document.

Description (in surveying): The exact delineation of land which identifies the intended premises.

Detail: The act of particularizing a portion of a plan in such a way as to expand it visually, showing greater visual completeness so as to reveal all characteristics of a portion of a plan. Failure to "detail" leads to claims by contractors against design professionals under an allegation that the plans and specifications were incomplete without greater detail.

Dictum: A statement by the court concerning application of law or a solution to a question raised by the case at bar that is used for illustration, argument or suggestion.

Dismissal: An order disposing of a cause of action without a trial of the allegation. Dismissals are granted in professional liability actions when the court is convinced that no cause of action lies against the defendant. Dismissal may be granted with prejudice, which means that the suit may not be brought against the same party for the same cause again; or without prejudice which prevents the decree of dismissal from barring a subsequent suit.

Domestic (underwriter): An underwriter whose domicile is in the United States.

Draftsman: Anyone who draws the schematic, tracings or plans of a building, facility, system, or equipment without rendering an engineering judgment. In insurance a "draftsman" is one who prepares plans and specifications, but does not visit a job site. In Workers' Compensation insurance, a licensed engineer may be called a "draftsman" even though his profession recognizes him as an engineer.

Drawings: The same as plans. Graphic or pictorial forms of a design concept. (See Specifications.)

Due Care: The duty that a reasonable and prudent man owes to others as respects his conduct. For the design professional, due care is the standard of care that would be exercised by the average reasonable man with the same special skills and knowledge, in the same or similar circumstances, performing in the same community. A breach of the duty of due care may be by affirmative act or the failure to act when under a duty to act. (See Negligence, Professional.)

Defamation: Statement damaging someone's reputation may embody the elements of both libel and slander. (See Libel and Slander hereafter.) A design professional may be defamed by allegations of inadquate professional performance if they are false and malicious.

Elevation (Surveying): Height above a fixed reference point, usually a bench mark or a datum point established by a governmental agency. Most bench marks are dated so as to indicate the time of establishing their position. This may be important in surveying since bench marks may settle and create inaccuracies. Surveys frequently make reference to the source of establishing height. Innacuracies in establishing correct elevation in land development can cause severe professional liability claims.

Employer (Workers' Compensation): One engaged in a business activity who has direction and control over another on his premises. Note: it is possible to become an employer of a person in some jurisdictions without intending to do so. "Premises" may mean anywhere a person practices his trade. For a design professional this may be at the job site as well as in his office. If a design professional exercises direction and control over another, he may inadvertently be considered his employer.

Employers' Liability: The liability imposed by law upon an employer for damages on account of bodily injuries, including death, sustained by an employee arising out of and in the course of his employment not otherwise covered by Workers' Compensation insurance. While claims under a doctrine of employers' liability are rare, they are a sufficient threat so that special coverage should be added to Workers' Compensation policies providing protection against them. Employers' Liability insurance is usually written in an annual aggregate amount which may vary by state.

Error: A mistake. A false conception. In engineering practice, "error" carries with it a connotation of being the result of professional negligence.

Errors and Omissions Insurance: See Professional Liability Insurance.

Estimate: A valuing of construction costs without actual measuring. A surmise as to cost of construction. While intended as a guide for the owner's use, an estimate is frequently mistaken for a warranty.

Evidence: Material used as legal proof. In professional liability, evidence is the data collected to substantiate a legal conclusion.

Excess Insurance: Insurance written to provide a higher limit than that provided by the primary insurance. Excess insurance goes into effect when the amount of loss covered by the primary insurance is exceeded.

Exclusion: A provision in an insurance contract limiting the scope of coverage by specifically withholding protection for described exposures.

Expert Witness: A person qualified to testify in regard to some professional or technical matter arising in a case. Such a person is permitted to give his opinion as well as state facts.

Extra: An addition to a project not contemplated in the original plans and specifications. Such addition usually results in added compensation for the contractor. Extras constitute a frequent source of professional liability claims; i.e., a contractor contends there are "extras" necessary since the plans and specifications did not clearly delineate the extent of the work.

Express Warranty: An explicit representation (often in writing) by a seller of goods and services made to the purchaser. (See Implied Warranty.)

F

Failure (Soil & Foundation Engineering): A landslide, cave-in, slump or other sudden, unusual and unexpected change in a land form.

Fault Doctrine: The theory of Common Law which stipulates that a party who is negligent and commits an error or omission which is injurious to another, is at fault and liable because of negligence. The fault doctrine is the basis used in professional liability claims. It is imperfect in that it fails to recognize that injuries occur in construction where there is little or no actual lack of due care on the part of those ultimately found liable. Courts and juries may create fictions in order to establish liability under this doctrine.

Federal Courts: The courts of United States Government. Few professional liability claims have been tried in Federal Courts. The results in Federal Courts have been more favorable to the design professional defendant, in most instances, than have the results in State Courts.

Floater Policy: An insurance policy which provides protection for items which are usually transportable.

Frivolous Suit: A suit which is brought clearly without basis in fact.

G

General Conditions: The main body of a building contract between owner and contractor that sets forth the duties and responsibilities of the parties.

Guarantee: A promise to be responsible for a level of performance of a duty, the quality of goods or the payment of some debt.

H

Hazard (Insurance): Risk or peril to be insured.

Hold Harmless or Hold Harmless & Indemnify: A contractual clause wherein one party agrees to indemnify another party for damages that are the result of certain contingencies. There are essentially three types of Hold Harmless and Indemnity clauses:
1. Limited — for the negligence of the indemnitor only.
2. Moderate — for the negligence of the indemnitor jointly with other parties.
3. Broad — For the sole negligence of the indemnitee without regard to the indemnitor's contribution.

Each jurisdiction of the United States has different rules governing the enforceability of Hold Harmless and Indemnity provisions. Both your attorney and your insurance broker should be consulted before any contract containing such a clause is signed. Many insurance policies exclude the assumption of liability under a Hold Harmless or Indemnity provision.

I

Implied Warranty: A warranty which is not expressed but arises from the intent of the parties. Breach of implied warranty is frequently charged in claims against design professionals. Most jurisdictions — though not all — will not sustain breach of implied warranty as a cause of action for claims against design professionals.

Improvement: An addition of value (more than a simple repair) affixed to real estate.

Indemnification: The act of indemnifying; the same as a hold harmless provision. Indemnification may be expressed, as in a contract; or implied, which is determined by a court.

Indemnity (Insurance): Payment made from an insurer to a claimant to make him whole from a loss; the money payment (plus cost of defense) from a liability policy that constitutes the total amount of the "loss." In Professional Liability Insurance, the money payment made by the underwriter to the claimant.

Insurance: A contract in which one party (the underwriter), in consideration of a premium paid, agrees with another party (the insured) to pay him or third parties a sum of money for damages or liability arising from a contingent event.

Inspection: Examination of construction to ensure that it conforms to the design concept expressed in the plans and specifications. This is the trade-meaning of the word. Legally, it is construed as a close, careful, critical examination. When using the term to describe a design professional's activities, care should be exercised to be certain that what is intended will not be misinterpreted.

Insurable Interest: A financial interest that would be lost or diminished due to damages or destruction. An interest in property such that a contract to indemnify against its loss will not be a wager; a financial interest in property. (Design professionals frequently have insurable interest upon a structure on which they have done a design prior to its completion or acceptance.)

J

Joint Venture: A mutual business undertaking in which two or more entities jointly share a voice in the control and a right to a portion of the profit or loss accruing from the undertaking. Care should be given in any association of two or more business entities so as to determine the nature of their relationship. Establishment of a joint venture has some far-reaching implications on Professional Liability, General Liability and Workers' Compensation Insurance. Joint ventures are separate legal entities within the eyes of the law. As such, they require their own insurance program. This is so even though it develops no separate payroll. Counsel with your attorney and insurance broker whenever you are involved with an association or collaborative undertaking with any other business entity in which you will share in the profit or losses.

K

Knowledge (Insurance): Information or belief of the truth. An understanding about a situation. This word is important in professional liability insurance since retroactive coverage will not be afforded to an insured for a claim arising out of an error, omission, or negligent act about which he had knowledge at the time coverage was bound. This means that extraordinary care should be taken to reveal the nature and extent of all pending disputes to the underwriter prior to the time coverage is bound.

L

Lapse (Insurance): To pass an insurance policy renewal date without reordering coverage, thus terminating coverage.

Legal Liability: An obligation enforceable by law.

Liability, Assumed: Liability undertaken by one party in a contract or an agreement which would normally have been the responsibility, in whole or in part, of a second party. (See Hold Harmless and Indemnity Agreement.)

Liability, Contingent: Liability arising out of the acts of others, not employees or agents.

Liability, Consequential: Liability which does not directly flow from the alleged error, omission or negligent act of the party, but is the result thereof. A failure in a design may make a building untenantable; the loss of rents would be considered consequential damages and would create consequential liability.

Liability, Derivative or Imputed: Liability coming to a party from the activities of others not under his direction and control.

Libel: A false, malicious expression in writing, printing or pictures which causes a person to be ridiculed, held in contempt or hated. Also, a publication, printing or picture which has a tendency to injure a person's professional status or professional confidence. (Similar to slander: Slander is spoken; libel is printed.)

Limit, Excess: A limit of insurance purchased over and above a basic limit in an insurance policy. Frequently two separate policies may be involved where an excess limit is purchased. This is sometimes referred to as "Layering" insurance limits. As many as four or five excess limits may be layered above the basic limit in order to give the required limit.

Liquidated Damages: A specific sum of money is expressly stipulated by the parties in a contract as damages are assessed against the contractor unless completion is accomplished on a certain day. Liquidated damage agreements pose a special problem for design professionals since the party called upon to pay them may try to recoup his loss by alleging that their performance impeded the progress of the work.

Litigation: A lawsuit; settlement of a dispute in a Court of Law.

Lloyds of London, or London (Insurance): An association of underwriting syndicates in London that have banded together under a common roof in order to provide insurance coverages. At Lloyds of London, each syndicate sits in a separate "box" and each underwrites a portion of a risk (percentage) until the total amount of needed insurance (100%) has been completed. Various underwriters may specialize in a line of insurance (a type of coverage) and take a "lead" on that line. The lead underwriter will usually take a major portion of the risk involved and other syndicates will subscribe below his signature ("underwrite") until the line is filled. The document they subscribe on is called "a line slip." Professional liability insurance for design professionals provided through Lloyds of London is written in this manner.

Locate (Surveying): To ascertain the correct position of a monument, or boundary marker. To decide upon the place a building or structure is to occupy.

M

Malpractice: Professional misconduct or the failure to use reasonable skill in the practice of professional duties; usually used in connection with medical practice. Also, professional misconduct toward a patient which is immoral or contrary to law.

Manufacture (Professional Liability): To produce an item on a mass production basis. Professional liability underwriters are loathe to insure design professionals who design items which may be "manufactured" for fear that an error in design may manifest itself repeatedly. In mass production, the potential damages are expanded commensurately.

Master Policy (Insurance): An insurance contract covering more than one risk as insureds. Usually certificates of insurance setting forth the terms and conditions of the master policy are issued to the individual risks that comprise the insureds under the master policy.

Material Representation (Insurance): Any statement of fact which is of sufficient importance that it affects the underwriting decision in a significant way. Any substantive statement about the insurability of a risk. Design professionals should be extremely cautious about the statements made on applications for professional liability insurance. They may be considered material representations. If they later prove to be inaccurate or false, the effectiveness of the coverage may be affected. (See Misrepresentation.)

Matter of Fact: In litigation, that which is determined concerning the physical progression of events leading to a loss. Determining matters of fact are frequently left to the jury.

Matter of Law: In litigations, determinations that are made by the applications of precedents, codes, and statutes. In suits, findings of fact are made and call for no special training or expertise. Findings of law are made based upon a body of knowledge learned by one trained to make such findings.

Misfeasance: A term used to describe the failure to properly perform a professional duty. Sometimes referred to as the omission to do a lawful act in a proper manner.

Misrepresentation (See Material Representation): A false and misleading statement which may cause a person to take a course of action in a contract which they would not have taken had the facts been known. If a misrepresentation is made in an application for insurance, and it is material to the underwriter's judgment as to the acceptability of a risk, such misrepresentation may be grounds for a recession of the contract or denial of liability if an insured loss occurs related to the material of misrepresentation.

Modification (Design): A change made in the plans and specifications usually found necessary during the course of construction. Modifications are made by the issuance of a written change order. A change order may contain both schematic and written instructions.

Monument (Surveying): A permanently established point of reference used in surveying. The monument is usually constructed to show an exact point for surveying purposes; however, monuments may be natural objects such as a tree, rock, or other natural and unmovable objects which may be used as a reference point. When this is done, the surveyor must exercise judgment as to the position of the point of reference on the natural object. Interpretation of the location of the actual monument may cause discrepancies in a survey with those made by another party. This fact gives rise to professional liability claims.

N

Negligence, Professional: The failure to exercise that degree of care in the conduct of professional duties that should be exercised by the average, prudent professional practicing in the same community under similar circumstances. For all practical purposes the "same community" is meaningless; modern transportation has largely removed community boundaries.

Negligence Per Se: Conduct which may be in violation of code, statute or safety orders that is in such clear violation of common prudence that it gives rise to a presumption of a breach of duty. This terminology is important to the design professional since, if negligence per se is established as respects his professional conduct, the burden of legal proof is shifted to him. In simple professional negligence, the plaintiff bears the burden of establishing that the design professional was professionally negligent.

O

Obiter Dictum: A remark made by the judge which is incidental to his decision; Latin, "by the way." In professional liability cases, the attitude of the court frequently is expressed in the "obiter dictum" or "dictum." This may presage a legal trend as respects professional liability claims since it demonstrates a state of mind.

Occurrence (Insurance): An accident, including injurious exposure to conditions, which results, during the policy period, in bodily injury or property damage, neither expected nor intended from the standpoint of the insured. This term contains some ambiguity since mistakes, in fact, may result in damage that is not "an accident" while the results may be unexpected, unforeseen, or have unusual consequences. A building that is misplaced due to inadvertent building across a property line, or the destruction of valuable foliage in order to make a survey are happenings which might not clearly fall within the intent of this term.

Or Equal: Equivalent: Having the same general attributes as another. This term is ambiguous in that when used in connection with certain construction components, it implies "exact duplication." This is not probable as between manufactured items. This term should be avoided where possible.

Owner: The person in whom title of property is vested. The word is frequently used to describe the person who has control, through ownership or otherwise, over a construction project.

Owner's or Contractor's Protective Liability Insurance: Insurance against liability imposed upon an owner or contractor for acts arising out of the operations of agents or subcontractors. This insurance is advisable for owners or contractors since they cannot always escape liability for acts of independent contractors whom they may hire. The very nature of construction is so hazardous that delegation to another party will not relieve a person for injuries resulting therefrom.

P

Package Deal: See Turnkey.

Partnership: A union of two or more parties for a business purpose. In a partnership one partner is liable for the liability arising from contract or tort caused by the other partner, so long as such liability was incurred while duties were being performed in behalf of the partnership. A joint venture is usually a special partnership; i.e., one formed for a job, as distinguished from general business. (See Joint Venture.)

Payee Clause: A clause in an insurance policy providing for payment of indemnity to a person other than the named insured because of a financial interest they may have in the insured subject matter.

Superintend: To have charge of something; implies direction and control over the manner of performing. In construction the design professional does not in any way "superintend" the performance of the work.

Subrogation: The right of an insurer to the insured rights against a third party for indemnification arising out of a payment.

Supervision: A term at one time used to describe the duties and responsibilities of a design professional observing the progress of the work in order to determine whether construction was proceeding in accordance with the plans and specifications. Now considered archaic. This term is now used only in connection with those having direction and control over the performance of the work. Unfortunately this term may inadvertently find its way into a design professional's contract.

Surveying: The setting of boundaries, measuring, mapping, construction staking, or other work performed by a surveyor. Care should be taken when using this term so that its ambiguity does not give rise to claims.

T

Testimony, Expert: Evidence given by a person who can demonstrate a special competence in a particular field; may be a judgment based upon experience.

Time of the Essence: A phrase used in contracts to establish that punctual performance is an essential element. Moderate delay in performance would be regarded as a violation of the contract. Design professionals should be extremely wary of any contract containing this term unless they are fully satisfied that they will be able to perform punctually.

Timely Delivery of Plans and Specifications (Professional Liability Insurance): Some professional liability insurance policies for design professionals contain an exclusion relating to the failure to make timely delivery of plans and specifications. A plaintiff may allege that failure to complete delivery on time has impeded the progress of the work and caused him to suffer damages. Claims of this nature may be made even though the design professional was in no way in control of certain factors which may have led to the delay; i.e., health, strike, weather, etc. Contracts imposing deadlines on the delivery of plans and specifications should be qualified so as to insure that the design professional will not be held responsible for conditions beyond his control.

Treaty Reinsurance: Reinsurance in which the reinsuring company agrees to reinsure all policies of a particular type for the company being reinsured. Reinsurance is purchased by most insurance companies to spread the possibility of a catastrophe loss, high frequency of claims, or an adverse loss ratio to other insurance companies.

Trespass: Entry on another person's real property without lawful authority. Civil engineers and land surveyors are particularly susceptible to claims based upon allegations of this unlawful act. Under certain circumstances, insurance may cover damages assessed against the offender committing trespass. Coverage varies with the circumstances and the **results** of the trespass.

Turnkey: An organization which performs both design and construction of a project. This terminology came from the suggestion that all duties, from concept until a key was turned in the door and handed to the owner, were performed by one entity. Design constructors are sometimes referred to as "turnkey."

U

Underwrite (Insurance): To provide insurance.

Unexpected (See Occurrence): With reference to causes of damage which could not have been foreseen.

V

Verdict: The formal findings made by a jury. A judgment may be predicated upon such findings. In rare instances a judgment may be rendered notwithstanding the verdict; i.e., contrary to the findings of the jury.

W

Waiver: The voluntary relinquishment of a known right sometimes in settlement of professional liability claims. The claimant may agree to waive claim in consideration for a reduction in fee. The document signed will be his voluntary relinquishment of claim.

Warranty, Express: An explicit statement in a contract usually made by the seller to a buyer. In insurance an agreement stated in the policy which requires that certain conditions be in effect if coverage is to be afforded; i.e., "The insured will drive only when sober."

Workers' Compensation: Payment required by state statutes of a fixed amount for injury to employees arising out of and in the course of their employment.

Workers' Compensation Insurance: Coverage issued for an employer in order to pay claims made by employees who may have been injured in the course of their employment. Coverage is effective for injury, sickness, and death, arising from employment. Most policies contain coverage for Common Law Employer's Liability as well as Workers' Compensation.

X

X.C.U. (Insurance): Coverage added to Comprehensive General Liability Insurance policies by endorsement providing protection against claims arising out of blasting, collapse and underground losses. Considered mandatory for contractors who may use explosives, excavate, or drill into the ground.

INDEX